THE PHILANTHROPIC RESULTS

OF

THE WAR IN AMERICA.

THE

PHILANTHROPIC RESULTS

OF

THE WAR IN AMERICA.

COLLECTED FROM

OFFICIAL AND OTHER AUTHENTIC SOURCES,

BY

An American Citizen.

Dedicated by permission to the United States Sanitary Commission.

NEW YORK:
SHELDON & Co., 335 Broadway; BOSTON, GOULD & LINCOLN;
LONDON, TRUBNER & Co.
1864.

PRESS OF WYNKOOP, HALLENBECK & THOMAS,
113 Fulton street, New York.

PREFACE.

In the summer of 1863, a merchant of New York, deeply impressed with the spirit of patriotism which had led the people of the loyal States to pour out their treasure and to give their personal service without stint for their country, was led to procure the preparation and publication of a pamphlet, on the philanthropic results of the war, for gratuitous circulation abroad. The eagerness with which our own citizens sought for copies of that pamphlet, which gave statistics of the contributions to the wants of our soldiers and their families to the spring of 1863, induced him to believe that a more extended and complete record of the nation's philanthropy in connection with the war would prove attractive and interesting. He has therefore caused the narrative and statistics to be brought up to February, 1864, and, taking advantage of the Metropolitan Fair for the benefit of the Sanitary Commission, has published a large edition, and presented it as his gift to the Commission. That it may stimulate the loyal hearts of the nation to acts of still greater sacrifice, and cause the fire of patriotism to burn with a yet higher and holier flame, is his earnest desire.

P. S.—In addition to those presented as above to the Commission, Messrs. Wynkoop, Hallenbeck & Thomas, the printers of this work, have generously donated one thousand copies to the Metropolitan Fair, and several other gentlemen a hundred or more copies each.

THE PHILANTHROPIC RESULTS

OF THE

WAR IN AMERICA.

CHAPTER I.

CONDITION OF THE COUNTRY AT THE COMMENCEMENT OF THE WAR.—SPONTANEOUSNESS OF THE CONTRIBUTIONS OF THE PEOPLE.—ADVANCES MADE BY THE STATE LEGISLATURES.—SUBSCRIPTIONS OF CITIES, BANKS, CORPORATIONS, AND PRIVATE CITIZENS.—CONTRIBUTIONS FOR ORGANIZING AND EQUIPPING REGIMENTS.—BOUNTIES RAISED BY STATES, COUNTIES, CITIES, TOWNS, AND PRIVATE CITIZENS, IN THE SUMMER OF 1862, AND SINCE THAT TIME.—MONEY EXPENDED FOR STATE DEFENSE.—APPROPRIATIONS MADE BY STATE LEGISLATURES FOR SICK AND WOUNDED SOLDIERS.

THE history of the benevolent enterprises growing out of the civil war has been so remarkable, so unlike anything in the previous experience of mankind, that it deserves a special record. Ordinarily, philanthropic efforts encounter, from their inception to their consummation, so much of the innate selfishness of our race, that a truthful narrative of their progress exhibits a succession of painful labors, on the part of those who seek to promote them, to convince those who are expected to contribute of the necessity of the case, and of their obligation to give; and while in a good cause the few give freely and heartily, the many only yield their dole to earnest and perhaps repeated solicitation. If the philanthropic work is one requiring continuous contributions from year to year, the solicitations must be repeated, with perhaps increasing urgency and vehemence of appeal, or the supply of means will diminish.

But in the philanthropic contributions made to objects connected with the present war, there has been such an abnegation of selfishness, such an earnest desire to give, such an unwillingness to be denied the privilege of giving, as have made the time an epoch in the history of benevolence. For about three years the calls on the liberality of the people have been increasing, and with every successive month they have increased almost in a geometric ratio ; but the calls have been met with so much promptness, and have so often been anticipated by their earnest zeal, that the greatest difficulty has been to direct the full flowing streams of charity into such channels as should most effectually and economically accomplish the objects desired by the liberal donors. To show how this has been done is our pleasing and grateful task.

The winter of 1860–61, had not been one of financial prosperity. Dark and threatening clouds hung over the nation's destiny. The Ship of State tossed on a stormy sea, and the arm of her pilot was neither steady nor strong. Traitors and mutineers were numerous in her crew, and some of them were high in command on her quarter-deck. The Secretary of the Treasury, a hearty sympathizer with the seceding States, and a few months later a general in the Rebel army, had so thoroughly impaired the national credit, that the Government six per cent. bonds, which at the beginning of his cabinet service he had bought up before maturity at 117, could not now be sold, even for a loan of ten millions, at 86. The Army was sent to remote points, the Navy carefully stationed on the other side of the globe; the arms intended for the use of the citizens of the Union in case of invasion or civil war delivered to the States which were now one after another marshaling themselves in rebellion to the Government, and the weak and selfish old man who was for the time Chief Magistrate, acknowledged himself powerless to breast the storm.

Business was paralyzed by the impending danger; the greater part of the Southern debtors repudiated their obligations to creditors at the North, either voluntarily or under the express command of their State Governments, and the losses thus sustained led to extensive bankruptcies. The day laborer, the artisan, the mechanic, the operatives from the manufactories, and the clerks from the stores sought employment, but in vain; there was not a full day's work for men in any department of labor except in tilling the soil.

It was in the midst of this horror of darkness that the proclamation of the President of the United States, announcing the fall of Fort Sumter, and calling for troops to defend the Capital from treason and rebellion, fell upon the nation's ear, and woke an instant response in the nation's heart.

There was no lack of men ready to peril their lives in the defense of their country ; the stagnation of business might in part account for this, but neither was there any lack of the necessary means for supplying the equipments, uniforms, and rations of the voluntary soldiers of the Republic. The national credit was indeed, as we have said, at a low ebb: incapacity and treason had brought it to this condition, but the Legislatures of most of the loyal States met in extra session, and without waiting to discuss the probability of their reimbursement by the National Government, voted with great unanimity large sums for arming and equipping troops. In some of the States the amounts thus voted were far beyond what they had ever dreamed of raising for State purposes. The aggregate amount thus advanced by the States within three weeks after the President's proclamation was $23,240,000, and within a year had reached the sum of $37,701,991. Of this sum about $12,000,000 was refunded to the States by the Government before July 1, 1862, and a portion of the remainder since that time. The border States, Delaware, Maryland, Kentucky, and Missouri, and the Pacific States, California and Oregon, did not at this time make any legislative grants, though in the summer, Kentucky and Missouri made appropriations for Home Guards.

The large sums thus voted for the opening of the war were not unwillingly contributed; on the contrary, men of all parties advocated the appropriations, and the people who must pay for these loans by heavy tax were more urgent than even their representatives that the grants should be liberal. The action of the Legislatures met a hearty approval at the ballot-box, and there were no complaints of heavy debt or oppressive taxation.

But it was not the State Legislatures alone which came forward thus promptly to aid the Government. Nearly every city and considerable town throughout the loyal States made its subscription, both by vote of its municipal authorities and by the spontaneous contributions of its business corporations and citizens. Before the 6th of May, 1861, New York city had contributed $2,173,000; Philadelphia, $330,000; Boston, $168,000;

Cincinnati, $280,000; Buffalo, $110,000; and other cities and towns in like proportion. An imperfect list, which gave the amounts contributed in less than half the cities and towns which had subscribed for the equipment of troops, showed an aggregate of $4,877,000. The entire amount considerably exceeded $7,000,000. From these two sources, then, in the first three weeks of the rebellion, a sum exceeding $30,000,000 was furnished toward the outfit of the volunteer army.

Was this vast outpouring of treasure by a people who, at the time, were suffering under financial disaster, the mad impulse of a sudden, frantic excitement, which soon passed away, leaving only regret for the extravagance it had prompted, or was it rather the deliberate action of a nation, to whom its institutions were dearer than life or property? The subsequent history of the war proves that the latter was the true explanation of this almost lavish liberality.

It was soon found that the task of quelling the Rebellion was one of gigantic proportions; that the conspirators had been for years maturing their plans, and that their treason could only be crushed out by the array of an overwhelming force. In his message of July 4th, President Lincoln suggested the propriety of calling for 400,000 men, and voting $400,000,000 for the work. Congress responded by authorizing calls for one million of men,* and $500,000,000. The work of raising and equipping such an army was entirely beyond the experience of any man in this country; beyond, indeed, the experience of any men of modern times; for large as some of the armies of modern Europe have been, no single power had ever called a million

* Congress probably intended to authorize the raising of only 500,000; but in reality, two separate acts, July 22, and July 25, were passed, each authorizing the raising of 500,000 men. Under these acts, 780,000 were actually raised.

of new troops into the field within a twelvemonth.

While the Government disbursed liberally for the bounties, uniforms, equipment, arming, and rations for these troops, there were other expenses connected with the organizations of the regiments which were met from private or municipal sources, of very large amount in the aggregate, larger in some regiments than others; but in those from Eastern States averaging somewhat more than $25,000 (some regiments cost over $75,000), and in the Western States from $15,000 to $20,000. The regiments thus raised to January, 1862, numbered somewhat more than eight hundred, and the amount paid by corporations, associations, and individuals, for recruiting purposes to that time, was not less than $16,000,000. From that period to January, 1864, over one thousand regiments have been raised, though at a somewhat smaller average expense. Careful inquiries indicate the present cost of placing a regiment in the field, aside from the Government expenditure, and bounties of all kinds at about $15,000. This would make the entire cost of recruiting borne by corporations, associations and individuals, between $31,000,000 and $32,000,000, which is probably a very low estimate.

The disasters which befell the Army of the Potomac, and the extraordinary exertions made by the Confederate authorities to call into the field as large a force as possible, led the President, in July, 1862, to issue a call for three hundred thousand three years' troops, and in August, a second, for three hundred thousand more, for nine months. An enrollment was ordered, preparatory to a draft, which it was supposed would be necessary for raising the second quota, but great exertions were made by the States, counties, and individuals, to encourage volunteering, by the offer of liberal bounties, extra pay, and provision for families, and in most of the States, these exertions were so far successful, that the quotas were nearly or quite filled without resort to conscription. The sums raised for bounties, &c., were in many of the States very large; in New York, the State offered a bounty of $50; the county of New York $50 additional, the county of Kings $60, and some of the other counties $75 or $100, while the subscriptions of wards, districts, and individuals, increased the amount in some instances to $250 or even $300. The average bounty paid in the State was computed to be over $150 per man, aside from that offered by the General Government. In several of the New England States this amount was exceeded. In Rhode Island, and in Massachusetts, and Connecticut, in many towns, the amount of bounty (with the State appropriation) was $300, $330, and in one or two cases as high as $375 per man, and the average for these three States was over $200. In Philadelphia an appropriation of $500,000 was made by the city, and a fund raised, by subscription, of $486,270.49 for the purpose of paying bounties, and aiding the families of the volunteers. In most of the Western States, very considerable sums were paid as bounties either by States, counties, towns, or cities. In many instances pledges were also given by wealthy citizens to pay specified sums monthly to the families of volunteers. In the State of New York, the amount thus paid for bounties and aid to families prior to July, 1863, by the State, counties, towns, cities, associations, and individuals, was not less than $17,500,000. In Connecticut it was nearly $6,000,000 ; in Massachusetts more than $7,500,000; in Vermont nearly $3,000,000. The lack of bureaux of military statistics in most of the States renders our information on these points indefinite, but when four of the loyal States, three of them small in territory, expended $34,000,000 for this purpose, it is not possible that the aggregate from all the loyal States could have fallen short of $55,000,000. The expiration of the term of service of the troops which had enlisted for two years, and of the nine months men, and the necessity for bringing into the field an army sufficiently formidable to crush the rebellion, which, though sorely crippled, was still rampant, led to the enactment of the enrollment, or as it is usually termed, the conscription act of March, 1863, and the proclamation of the President of a draft for 300,000 men in May, 1863. Volunteering for the filling up of the old regiments and the organization of new ones had been progressing, though slowly, through the winter and spring. The draft did not yield so large a force as was expected: only about 50,000 of those drawn, serving either in person or by substitute; and the formation of veteran regiments composed of those who had been for one year or more in the service, was resolved on. The United States

Government offered the liberal bounty of $402 to each man who should re-enlist. In October, 1863, the Government called for 300,000 volunteers, offering the same bounty to those who had already served, or $302 to new recruits, and in January, the President increased the call to 500,000, of which, however, the drafted men, and those enlisted under the call of October, were to form a part. The regiments whose term of service would expire in the spring of 1854, were allowed to re-enlist, and receive the bounty if they chose, and form a portion of the new force. In default of a sufficient number of volunteers being secured by April, the enrollment act, modified by Congress, was to be enforced, and a draft proclaimed. These measures led to renewed exertions to stimulate volunteering, both for the purpose of avoiding the draft, and to fill up as speedily as possible the wasted numbers of the armies in the field. The terrible battles of Chancellorsville, Gettysburgh, and Stone River, the sieges of Vicksburg and Port Hudson, and the severe engagement of Chickamauga, and the battles around Chattanooga, had occasioned great loss of life, and had permanently disabled many thousands for future service. Probably not less than 100,000 Union soldiers were *hors du combat* from these and other engagements of the year. The rebels, meanwhile, were straining every nerve, and by the most relentless conscription were forcing every man between the ages of 17 and 60 into their ranks, and nothing short of the utmost exertion would enable the Government to meet them with equal numbers.

To facilitate volunteering by increasing still further the liberal bounties offered by the Government was seen to be the dictate alike of patriotism and sound policy, and the State Legislatures, counties, cities, towns, and individuals again contributed largely to this object. In the State of New York, the Legislature appropriated $8,841,098; Boards of Supervisors, $13,033,291.75; Common Councils $3,079,608.50; and towns and individuals about $4,000,000 more, making a sum total of $28,953,998.45, from that State alone. Massachusetts paid $7,625,436; Connecticut, $2,000,000; Vermont, $2,000,000, Iowa, $1,250,000; Indiana, $3,500,000, and other States in like proportion. The aggregate of the bounties thus paid, aside from those allowed by the General Government, exceeded $75,000,000.

There had been also expended during this period, by particular States, large sums for State defense or protection against dangers which threatened them individually; thus Maine, Massachusetts, and New York had made appropriations for harbor and coast defense and State war vessels. Pennsylvania, for harbor defense and protection of her southern line against invasion, and had, besides, met with very heavy losses in consequence of the rebel invasion in the summer of 1863; Ohio, Indiana, and Illinois had raised troops for defense of the Ohio river frontier. Kentucky, Missouri, and Maryland had raised and maintained considerable bodies of Home Guards and local militia for service in protecting their States from the marauding bands of the rebels; and Iowa and Minnesota had raised troops to put down the Indians who had risen upon the whites in those States. The militia of Maryland, Pennsylvania, New Jersey, New York, and Ohio had also been called out to the number of 100,000, to repel the invasion of Pennsylvania and Maryland, in June, 1863, and though they were paid by the United States Government while in actual service, the expenditures for their outfit, &c., came upon the States. The aggregate expenditure for these purposes, as nearly as can be ascertained, was about $12,000,000, without taking into account the losses of private property by the rebels and the Indians.

In many of the States, special appropriations were made or a contingent fund allowed to the Governor to be used for the relief of sick and wounded soldiers, either in hospitals, on the field, or on their way home. These appropriations amounted to about $900,000.

CHAPTER II.

CONTRIBUTIONS FOR THE COMFORT OF SOLDIERS AND THE RELIEF OF THEIR FAMILIES.—THE "UNION VOLUNTEER REFRESHMENT SALOON" AND THE "COOPER SHOP REFRESHMENT SALOON," OF PHILADELPHIA.—THE "UNION RELIEF ASSOCIATION," OF BALTIMORE.—THE "SUBSISTENCE COMMITTEE," OF PITTSBURG.—OTHER SIMILAR ORGANIZATIONS ELSEWHERE.—THE SIMULTANEOUS IMPULSE TO WORK FOR THE SOLDIERS, AT THE OPENING OF THE WAR.—THE WOMAN'S CENTRAL ASSOCIATION OF RELIEF IN NEW YORK.—THE ORIGIN OF THE UNITED STATES SANITARY COMMISSION.—ITS PROPOSED SPHERE OF ACTION.—DR. WOOD'S APPLICATION IN ITS BEHALF—AUTHORIZATION BY THE SECRETARY OF WAR AND THE PRESIDENT.—ITS CONSTITUENT MEMBERS.

THE cry that the Capital was in danger, echoed through the land after the memorable proclamation of the President on the 15th of April, 1861, and the volunteer soldiery who rallied at once for its protection against the treasonabledesigns of the rebels, came forward in such haste that, in many cases, they were not provided with sufficient rations or necessary change of apparel. To provide these for them tasked the utmost energies of the patriotic men and women of the country, Everywhere the sewing-machines, those "swift-fingered sisters of charity," were driven at their utmost speed, and paused not even for the rest of the Sabbath, in preparing needful articles of clothing, and the needle-women, scarcely less swift in their labors of love, worked till the gray dawn streaked the east, and after the briefest possible interval of rest, returned anew to their toil. Food was prepared in immense quantities, but still not enough for the hungry mouths to be filled, and while all deemed it a privilege to do what they could for the soldier, the want of system and organization in the work was such that there was danger, after all, that some would suffer. As a matter of fact, some did suffer. The regiments which poured in quick succession from the Eastern States into New York, and from that city into Philadelphia, were not only, as was inevitable, crowded in too large numbers upon the transport ships, but they were often for twenty-four hours or more without food. The spontaneous instincts of patriotism among the working classes in the vicinity of the landings, in both cities, exhibited itself in hastening to the cars with food from their own scanty stores to appease the hunger of these famishing citizen soldiers In Philadelphia, the efforts of a few generous but humble souls thus to supply the wants of the volunteers gradually grew up into organized institutions of relief and refreshment. At first, it was a poor man boiling coffee for the soldiers on the sidewalk, and his neighbors, as poor as himself, hastening with their loaves of bread, their slices of bacon, and other articles of food, to the wharves, whenever the signal-gun told of the arrival of a regiment; ere long there were two bands vieing with each other in their care for the regiments which continued to come, oftenest at night, on their way to the theatre of war. One occupied a portion of a large cooper-shop, the other an old boat-house, and by and by, as their quarters grew too small, other buildings were added, and among them, small hospitals for the soldiers taken sick on their journey. Thus grew up, in a rivalry of good works, the Union Volunteer Refreshment Saloon, and the Cooper-shop Refreshment Saloon, both consecrated to the service of supplying freely the wants of the soldiers in transit to and from the army of the Potomac. The citizens of Philadelphia have contributed liberally and heartily to the support of both, and the committees of both organizations, composed almost wholly of men and women of the working classes, have toiled indefatigably for nearly three years, often laboring through nearly the whole night in the preparation of meals, to have them ready for the soldiers on their arrival. One of these institutions (the Union Volunteer Refreshment Saloon) reports the furnishing of 400,000 meals to soldiers, the dressing of the wounds or medical attendance upon over 10,000 sick and wounded soldiers, and the furnishing of lodgings to about 20,000 This has been accomplished from the expenditure of about $40,000 in money and $17,000 in sanitary stores and provisions. The other, the Cooper-shop Refreshment Saloon, to December, 1863, had expended $40,232.22 in money, and had fed 214,169 soldiers. They had given temporary attention to the wounds of a large number of soldiers in transit, and had had over 600 under treatment in their hospital.

The heroic and protracted sacrifices made by the excellent people who have consecrated themselves to these blessed labors of charity and love of country, are deserving of being held in everlasting remembrance. The example thus set was very soon imitated in other cities. Baltimore, whose Union men had, at first, to resist the flood of disloyalty which swept over the city, and stained it with the blood of some of the noblest sons of Massachusetts, was the foremost in this work. Her Union citizens were tried and true, and in the month of May, 1861, they began, in a humble way at first, to provide for the wants of the soldiers who passed through the city, amid much obloquy and reproach; but soon gaining strength, they organized the Union Relief Association, and up to the 25th of June 1863, had fed 451,639 soldiers and expended in this work of benevolence, $61,693.49. Nowhere in the Union does the fire of patriotism and philanthropy burn with an intenser and purer flame than in Baltimore. A similar organization, called the "Pittsburgh Subsistence Committee," was established very early in the war at Pittsburgh. Up to June, 1863, over 200,000 soldiers had been fed by it. At Cincinnati, Louisville, and St. Louis, organizations of an analogous character were established in the summer of 1861.

The proclamation of the President, as we have already intimated, evoked the patriotic and earnest sympathies of the women of the nation, as well as those of the sterner sex. Everywhere fair hands were at work, and fair brows grew grave with thought, of what could be done for those who were going forth to fight the nation's battles. With the characteristic national fondness for organization, Ladies' Aid and Relief Societies were formed everywhere. One, "The Soldiers' Aid Society," at Cleveland, Ohio, bearing date April 20, 1861, only five days after the President's proclamation; another at Philadelphia, "The Ladies' Aid Society," adopting its constitution on the 26th of April, and a third, "The Woman's Central Association of Relief, of New York," on the 30th of the same month. By the middle of May there were hundreds of these associations formed. As yet, however, they hardly knew what was to be done, or how, when, and where to do it That lint was to be scraped, bandages prepared, socks knit, flannel shirts made, and other work of a similar kind performed, they were aware, but what further was to be done, and how the articles prepared were to be distributed to the army without waste, was a matter of uncertainty. There was a strong impulse on the part of many of the younger ladies to devote themselves to the work of nursing the sick and wounded; the noble deeds of Florence Nightingale had surrounded her with a halo of saintliness which they would give life itself to win, but most of them knew little of the arduous duties of a hospital nurse, and, as yet, happily, there were very few sick and no wounded to be nursed. The Woman's Central Association of Relief had among its officers some gentlemen of large experience in sanitary science, and of considerable knowledge of military hygiene, and they wisely gave a practical turn to its labors from the first. Those who desired to become army nurses were required to pass examination as to their qualifications, and then to attend a course of instruction and training at one of the hospitals and under the direction of eminent physicians, for their duties. The Association was apprised that its first duty was to ascertain what the Government would and could do, and then help it by working with it, and doing what it could not do. Other organizations of gentlemen were attempting by different, yet in the main, similar measures, to render assistance to the Government. Among these were the "Advisory Committee of the Board of Physicians and Surgeons of the Hospitals of New York," and "The New York Medical Association for furnishing Hospital Supplies in aid of the Army," both new associations, called into existence by the exigencies of the war. Fraternizing with each other, as they well might, since they all looked to the accomplishment of the same end, these associations resolved to send a joint delegation to Washington, to confer with the Government, and ascertain by what means they might best co-operate with it, for the benefit of the soldiers of the nation.

On the 18th of May, 1861, Messrs. Henry W. Bellows, D. D., W. H. Van Buren, M. D., Elisha Harris, M. D., and Jacob Harsen, M. D., representatives of these three associations, drew np and forwarded to the Secretary of War a communication setting forth the propriety of creating an organization which should unite the duties and labors of three associations, and co-operate with the Medical Bureau of the War Department to such an extent that each might aid the other in securing the welfare of the army. For this purpose they asked that a mixed commission of civilians, military officers, and medical men, might be appointed by the Government, charged with the duty of methodizing and reducing to practical service the already active but undirected benevolence of the people towards the army, who should consider the general subject of the prevention of sickness and suffering among the troops, and suggest the wisest method which the people at large could use to manifest their good-will towards the comfort, security, and health of the army. They referred to the commissions which followed the Crimean and Indian wars, and brought to light the vast amount of suffering which had been needlessly endured there, and begged that, in this case, the organization might *precede* the war, and prevent so far as possible the suffering which would otherwise ensue. They suggested, also, the appointment of cooks and nurses for the army, and stated that the "Woman's Central Association of Relief" stood ready to undertake the training of both in their duties.

On the 22d of May, R. C. Wood, M. D., then Acting Surgeon-General, now in charge of the Western Medical Department, followed this communication by a letter addressed to the Secretary of War, urging the establishment of the desired Commission as a needed adjunct to the new, extensive, and overwhelming duties of the Medical Bureau.

On the 23d of May, the delegation addressed to the Secretary of War, a " Draft of powers, asked from the Government, by the Sanitary delegates to the President and Secretary of War." In this paper the powers desired, were stated as follows :

"1.The Commission being organized for the purposes only of inquiry and advice, asks for no legal powers, but only the official recognition and moral countenance of the Government, which will be secured by its public appointment. It asks for a recommendatory order, addressed in its favor to all officers of the movement, to further its inquiries ; for permission to correspond and confer, on a confidential footing, with the Medical Bureau and the War Department, proffering such suggestions and counsel as its investigations and studies, may from time to time, prompt and enable it to offer.

"2. The Commission seeks no pecuniary remuneration from the Government. Its motives being humane and patriotic, its labors will be its own reward. The assignment to them of a room in one of the public buildings, with stationery and other necessary conveniences, would meet their expectations in this direction.

"3. The Commission asks leave to sit through the war, either in Washington, or when and where it may find it most convenient and useful; but it will disband should experience render its operations embarrassing to the Government, or less necessary and useful than it is now supposed they will prove."

Concerning the objects of the Commission, the delegation say ·

"The general object of the Commission is through suggestions reported from time to time, to the Medical Bureau and the War Department, to bring to bear upon the health, comfort and *morale* of our troops, the fullest and ripest teachings of sanitary science, in its application to military life, whether deduced from theory or practical observations, from general hygienic principles, or from the experience of the Crimean, the East India, and the Italian wars. Its objects are purely advisory."

They indicate the following specific objects of inquiry:

"1. *Materiel of the Volunteers.* The Commission proposes a practical inquiry into the material of the Volunteer forces, with reference to the laws and usages of the several States, in the matter of inspections, with the hope of assimilating the regulations with those of the army proper alike in the appointment of medical and other officers, and in the vigorous application of just rules and principles to recruiting and inspection laws. This inquiry would exhaust every topic appertaining to the original *materiel* of the army, considered as a subject of sanitary and medical care.

II. *Prevention.* The Commission would inquire with scientific thoroughness into the subject of diet, cooking, cooks, clothing, huts, camping grounds, transports, transitory depots, with their expenses, camp police, with reference to settling the question, how far the regulations of the army proper, are or can be practically carried out among the volunteer regiments, and what changes or modifications are desirable from their peculiar character and circumstances? Everything appertaining to outfit, cleanliness, precautions against damp, cold, heat, malaria, infection and unvaried or ill cooked food, and an irregular or careless commissariat, would fall under this head.

"III. *Relief.* The Commission would inquire into the organization of Military Hospitals,general and regimental; the precise regulations and routine through which the services of the patriotic women of the country may be made available as nurses; the nature and sufficiency of hospital supplies; the method of obtaining and regulating all other extra and unbought supplies, contributing to the comfort of the sick; the question of ambulances and field services, and of extra medical aid; and whatever else relates to the care, relief, or cure of the sick and wounded, their investigations being guided by the highest and latest medical and military experience, and carefully adapted to the nature and wants of our immediate army, and its peculiar origin and circumstances."

The President and Secretary of War were not at first disposed to look with any great favor upon this plan, which they regarded rather as a sentimental scheme concocted by women, clergymen, and humane physicians, than as one whose practical workings would prove of incalculable benefit to the army which was rapidly coming into existence. The earnestness of its advocates, their high position, and the evidence which was adduced that they only represented the voice of the nation, produced some effect in modifying their views, and when the Acting Surgeon-General asked for it, as a needed adjuvant to the Medical Bureau, likely soon to be overwhelmed by its new duties, they finally decided, though reluctantly, to permit its organization.

Accordingly the Secretary of War, on the 9th of June, decided on the creation of such a Commission, the President approving. The title first given to the new organization was "The Commission of Inquiry and Advice in respect of the Sanitary Interests of the United States Forces," but was subsequently changed to "The United States Sanitary Commission."

It was composed of the following gentlemen: Rev. Henry W Bellows, D. D.,

President, New York; Professor A. D. Bache, Vice President, Washington; Elisha Harris, M. D., Corresponding Secretary, New York; George W. Cullum, U. S. A., Washington; Alexander E. Shiras, U. S. A., Washington; Robert C. Wood, M. D., U. S. A., Washington; William H. Van Buren, M. D., New York; Wolcott Gibbs, M. D., New York, Cornelius R. Agnew, M. D., New York; George T. Strong, New York; Frederick Law Olmsted, New York; Samuel G. Howe, M. D., Boston; J. S. Newberry, M. D, Cleveland, Ohio. To these were subsequently added Horace Binney, Jr., Philadelphia; Rt. Rev. Thomas M. Clark, D. D., Providence, R. I.; Hon. Joseph Holt, Kentucky; R. W. Burnett, Cincinnati, Ohio; Hon. Mark Skinner, Chicago, Illinois; Rev. John H. Heywood, Louisville, Kentucky; Professor Fairman Rogers, Philadelphia; J. Huntington Wolcott, Boston; and about five hundred associate members, in all parts of the country.

CHAPTER III.

THE UNITED STATES SANITARY COMMISSION CONTINUED.—ITS ORGANIZATION.—ITS MEDICAL PUBLICATIONS.—ITS SERVICES IN THE FIELD.—THE THREE DEPARTMENTS OF THE SANITARY COMMISSON'S WORK.—I. SANITARY INSPECTION OR PREVENTIVE SERVICE.—ITS SUBDIVISIONS.—II. GENERAL RELIEF.—HOW ADMINISTERED.—III. SPECIAL RELIEF.—HOMES.—LODGES.—HOSPITAL DIRECTORY.—OTHER MODES OF SPECIAL RELIEF.—RECEIPTS OF THE COMMISSION.—IN MONEY.—IN SUPPLIES.—THE LATTER DRAWN FROM THE BRANCHES.—SANITARY FAIRS.—THE WESTERN SANITARY COMMISSION.—ITS ORGANIZATION.—ITS WORK.—ITS RECEIPTS.

IT is a matter of wonder, that in a field so wholly new the delegation should have so fully comprehended the duties which would be incumbent upon the Commission, and the range of its future operations. There were indeed certain features of its work which, of necessity, could only be developed by the bitter experiences through which it was called to pass; and in the end, the great lack in the Government Medical Service, compelled it to assume more of the executive and less of the advisory functions. Still it has never failed to bear in mind that it was created to aid by its advice, counsel, and where needed, its direct help, the medical department of the Government service, and has ever been ready to withdraw from every duty which that Department, under its constantly increasing efficiency, could successfully perform.

Under its charter, it at once proceeded to organize its action and to appoint committees from its members to visit every camp, recruiting-post, transport, fort, hospital, and military station, to ascertain and report all abuses, and to perfect such organization as might insure a higher degree of health and comfort for the soldiers.

The medical members of the Commission undertook to consider the questions which might arise concerning the diseases of the camp, and their medical and surgical treatment, from the highest scientific point of view, and guided by the rich and abundant experience of

European army surgeons, to prepare brief medical and surgical tracts adapted to the wants of the volunteer surgeons of the Army. Among these tracts, of which many thousands have been circulated, were "Advice as to Camping;" "Report on Military Hygiene and Therapeutics;" "Dr. Guthrie's Directions to Army Surgeons on the battle-field;" "Rules for preserving the Health of the Soldier;" "Quinine as a prophylactic against malarious Diseases;" "Report on the value of Vaccination in armies;" "Report on Amputation;" "Report on Amputation through the foot and at the ancle joint;" "Report on Venereal Diseases;" "Report on Pneumonia;" "Report on Continued Fevers;" "Report on Excision of Joints for traumatic cause;" "Report on Dysentery;" "Report on Scurvy;" "Report on the Treatment of Fractures in military surgery;" "Report on the nature and treatment of Miasmatic Fevers;" "Report on the treatment of Yellow

Fever;" "Report on the treatment of Infectious Diseases," &c. It is no more than justice to the able authors of these essays, to say that they take rank with the best medical and surgical treatises extant, and have been of incalculable value to the surgeons in whose hands they have been placed.

Three important committees were appointed, one to communicate the matured counsels of the Commission to the Government, and procure their ordering by the proper Departments; a second to maintain a direct relation with the army officers and medical men, with the camps and hospitals, and by all proper methods to make sure of the carrying out of the sanitary orders of the Medical Bureau and the War Department; and a third to be in constant communication with the State Governments, and the public benevolent associations interested in the army.

This plan of organization was approved

by the Secretary of War, on the 13th June, 1861, and on the 21st of that month the Commission issued its first address to the public. This was soon followed by an eloquent appeal to the Life Insurance Companies, and another to men of wealth throughout the country for aid in the prosecution of its work. The members of the Commission, as such, received no compensation, but the purposes of the organization would require a very considerable number of paid employés, and would involve heavy expenses for publications and supplies, which could only be purchased with money. A considerable number of associate members were elected at this time, who gave their services in raising means for the operations of the Commission, and Ladies' Associations, in all parts of the country, prepared clothing and supplies of all sorts, and forwarded them to its depots.

The members of the Commission visited, during the summer of 1861, the *different camps of the widely-extended* armies of the Republic, and carefully inspected and reported upon their sanitary condition and needs.

The necessity of the services of the agents of the Commission on the field immediately after, or when practicable, during the progress of, important battles, was felt, as soon as such battles occurred. At first, owing to the difficulties of procuring transportation for its supplies to the field, in consequence of the dependence of the Medical Bureau upon the Quartermaster's Bureau for transportation, it could not reach the field so early as its officers desired, and in some of the earlier battles, there was great suffering (partially ameliorated, it is true, by individual effort and enterprise), in consequence. But the Commission soon found it necessary to have its own independent transportation, and this both by land and water; its hospital transports, its wagons and ambulances, and its ambulance railroad cars. In July, 1863, it added to these the plan of attaching to each army corps a Superintendent of Relief, with his assistants, wagons, ambulances, and supplies, to remain constantly with his corps and minister to its needs.

It has, throughout, worked in harmony with the United States Government, and especially with the Medical Bureau, to which it has proved of great service. That bureau, which, at the commencement of the war, was utterly inadequate, though from no fault of its own, to the vast work before it, is now well regulated and admirably organized, having a corps of three thousand skillful and responsible surgeons, and fifteen thousand hired nurses experienced in their duties.

But even with this large force, trained as it has been by the arduous duties to which it has been called, there are, and must be, numerous instances where the most perfect working of the Government machinery cannot remedy suffering and misery which a more flexible system can relieve. The presence of incipient scurvy among the troops on Morris Island, and the forces engaged in the siege of Vicksburg and Port Hudson, was detected and remedied by the sending at once of large amounts of fresh vegetables and anti-scorbutics by the Commission to those points, which reached them promptly, and arrested the disease, while, by the necessarily slow movements of the Government, many weeks must have elapsed ere the needed remedies could have been furnished, and meantime half the forces engaged would have perished. "Potatoes and onions," says one of the energetic lady agents of the Commission in Chicago, "captured Vicksburg." "The supplies of fresh vegetables and anti-scorbutics sent by the Sanitary Commission to Morris Island, saved the army of the South," is the testimony of an impartial but thoroughly competent witness, who spent ten months in the hospitals of that department in 1863.

The work of the Sanitary Commission now comprehends the following distinct departments of labor: 1st. *The preventive service or Sanitary Inspection*, which requires a corps of Medical Inspectors, whose time is passed with each army corps in the field, visiting camps, hospitals, and transports; skillful and experienced physicians, who watch the perils from climate, malarious exposure, from hard marching or active campaigning, from inadequate food or clothing, growing out of imperfect facilities of transportation, and report to the Chief Inspector of that army, and through him to the Chief of Inspection at Headquarters, for remedy, or to the Associate Secretary in charge, or to Relief Agents under their control, and thus see to the supplying of the needs of that portion of the army, and the adoption of the necessary measures for the improvement of its sanitary condition. From the reports of these Inspectors the materials are gathered which are digested into such forms as to be of permanent value in the Commission's Bureau of Statistics. To this department belongs also the corps of Special Hospital Inspectors, selected from the most learned and skillful physicians of the country, who, from time to time, make the circuit of all the general hospitals of the army, (now 233 in number), and report upon their wants, condition, progress, *personnel*, and capacity for improvement. The substance of these reports is confidentially made over to the Surgeon-General. A third agency, in connection with this preventive service, is the preparation and circulation of medical tracts, and information important and indispensable to the officers, soldiers, and especially the medical men in the field. The titles of these medical tracts we have already given, but the Commission has also published many giving important suggestions to the officers and men, not properly medical in their character.

II. *The Department of General Relief.*—The supplies of food, clothing, bandages, hospital furniture, clothing, and bedding, delicacies for the sick, stimulants and cordials, for the wounded on the field, the sick and wounded in camp, field, regimental, post, and general hospitals, come from the branches of the Commission, of which there are twelve, having depots in Boston, New York, Philadelphia, Baltimore, Cincinnati, Cleveland, Chicago, Buffalo, Pittsburg, Detroit, Columbus, and Louisville. Each of these branches, which are variously denominated as Ladies' Aid Societies, Relief Associations, &c., has its distinctly defined field, from which it draws its supplies, and has from one hundred and fifty to twelve hundred auxiliary aid societies, in the towns, hamlets, and villages, and, in the cities, in the different churches, of its field. The stores collected by the branch are received at its depot, opened, assorted, each kind by itself, repacked, and reports of the number and amount of the supplies thus accumulated, are sent every week to the principal office of the Commission, or to the Associate Secretary of the Eastern or Western Department, as the case may be, and shipped, according to orders received, to the army where they are needed, with the utmost promptness. One of these branches (the "Woman's Central Association of Relief") reported, among the stores forwarded from its depot, from May 1, 1861, to Nov. 1, 1863, 471,318 pieces of clothing, 291,810 pieces of bedding, and over 85,000 packages of fruit, vegetables, jellies, wine, condensed milk, beef-stock, groceries, pickles, lemonade, &c., of a total value of $566,831.14, beside $35,551.38 in money. The supplies thus furnished are distributed with great care to avoid waste, and to supplement the food, clothing, and medicines which the Government is bound to furnish—the object being to do what the Government cannot, and to avoid duplicating its supplies of what it can and should furnish. Care is exercised also to avoid imposition, while no sufferer in need is allowed to suffer when the Commission can supply his wants. The Commission is national in its character, and supplies the soldiers of one State as readily as those of another. Nay, more: the rebel wounded, when left on the field, or in temporary hospitals within the Union lines, or when sent to camps and hospitals as prisoners, have uniformly received its bounty and its assiduous care. It has had in this matter, at times, to contend, both among the people and on the field, with that exclusive feeling which would limit its beneficence to the soldiers of a single State or regiment; but oftenest the agents of these local organizations have, from the feeling which such exclusiveness has caused among the soldiers, turned their stores into the depots of the Commission, and themselves aided in their distribution to the soldiers, without distinction of locality. The Field Relief

Superintendents, already mentioned, who accompany each army corps, belong to this department of general relief.

III. *The Department of Special Relief.*—This department is under the general superintendence of Rev. F. N. Knapp, Associate Secretary of the Commission for the East, at Washington, and of Dr. J. S. Newberry, Associate Secretary for the West, at Louisville. It furnishes homes to soldiers, where shelter, food, and medical care and general superintendence are furnished for those soldiers who are not yet under the care of the Government, or have just got out of their care, or have somehow lost their status and cannot immediately regain it—recruits, or men on leave, sick leave or furlough, going to and fro; men without skill to care for themselves, ignorant, underwitted, or vicious; men discharged prematurely from the hospitals; men found in the streets, or left behind by their regiments. Of these classes, about 2,300 are accommodated daily or nightly in the homes of the Commission at Washington, Cincinnati, Cairo, Louisville, Nashville, Columbus, Cleveland, and New Orleans.

There are also belonging to this department five lodges—homes on a smaller scale—where the wearied soldier, sick or feeble, may await his opportunity of obtaining his pay, from the Paymaster-General, or landing sick from a steamer or cars, and unable to reach the hospital to which he may belong, can find rest, food, and medical care, till he can be transferred to the hospital, or is able to rejoin his regiment. There are now two of these at Washington, one at Alexandria, one at Memphis, and one at Vicksburg; and others are established temporarily, as occasion may require, at other points. The hospital cars, of which there are several, between Washington and New York, and between Louisville and Murfreesboro', Tennessee, fitted up with hammocks in rubber slings, and with a small kitchen for preparing the necessary food for the sick and wounded, and under the charge of a skillful surgeon, belong to this department; as do also the Sanitary steamers, the Clara Bell, on the Mississippi, the New Dunleith, on the Cumberland, and the Elizabeth, on the Potomac. These are used both for the transmission of necessary supplies, and the transportation of the wounded. In this department, also, the Commission have established agencies at Washington, Philadelphia, and New York, for obtaining for the soldiers, and their families, pensions, bounties, back pay, transportation, aid in correcting the soldiers' papers, where there are errors in form, or recovering them their positions when they have wrongfully been set down as deserters, and saving them from sharpers. The Commission have also established Hospital Directories at Washington, Philadelphia, New York, and Louisville. In these four directories are registered the names of all soldiers in the two hundred and thirty-three hospitals, and as far as possible, the regimental and post hospitals throughout the country, and these are constantly receiving additions from the reports sent regularly from such hospitals. By applying to these Directories, information will be furnished to friends without cost, other than that of postage or telegram, of the location and condition of any soldier who is or has been within a year, an inmate of any U. S. military hospital. At the Washington office of the Commission, the names of patients in the hospitals in Eastern Virginia, Maryland, District of Columbia, North Carolina, South Carolina, Florida, and Louisiana, are recorded ; at Philadelphia, those in Pennsylvania hospitals ; at New York, those in New York, New Jersey, and New England ; at Louisville, those in Western Virginia, Ohio, Indiana, Illinois, Missouri, Iowa, Kentucky, Tennessee, Mississippi, and Arkansas. The officers in charge require the name, rank, company, and regiment of the person inquired for, and where he was when last heard from. About 550,000 names have been thus recorded, and the information afforded by these directories to the friends of the sick and wounded has been of incalculable value, often leading to the preservation of life, and to the relief of that most terrible mental anguish, the torture of a dread uncertainty.

Still another measure of special relief, on which the Commission has expended more than $30,000, is the sending of supplies, so long as it was permitted, to our soldiers who were prisoners at Richmond, and there undergoing the terrors of cold, nakedness, and starvation. It also sent on every flag-of-truce boat from Fortress Monroe, ample stores of clothing, cordials, nourishing food, medicine, and restoratives, for the poor fellows who were exchanged, and who, but for this timely relief, would have many of them died on the voyage. It has organized a system of furnishing fresh supplies to the hospitals around Washington at prime cost, which it brings from Philadelphia in arctic cars, thus preventing frauds and the commissions formerly obtained by the hospital stewards, and furnishing more and better supplies to the inmates of the hospitals for less money. It has caused reforms to be instituted in our own convalescent and parole camps, and in the prison camps of the rebels, which our Government hold as prisoners, promoting the health and comfort of both in every possible way. Its agents and superintendents have often brought off men under fire from the battle-field, and four of them were taken prisoners by the rebels, after Gettysburg, and notwithstanding the kindnesses bestowed by the Commission on rebels, wounded and prisoners, were subjected to the meagre fare and intolerable filth of Libby prison and Castle Thunder, for months, when two of them were finally released on parole.

In these labors it has constantly had the aid and co-operation of the Medical Department, and where it could be bestowed, that of the Quartermaster's Department, and the generals and commanding officers in the field have, almost without exception, given it their hearty sanction and assistance. Without these, its work would have been fourfold more expensive than it has, but even with this assistance, it has necessarily had to incur large expenditures, and has distributed supplies to an immense value. At the commencement of its work, when it was expected that the war would be a brief one it made its appeals to the public for fifty thousand dollars, a sum which it was thought would suffice to accomplish its purposes; but with the increasing proportions of the war, increasing means were found necessary. While, of most descriptions of supplies, their stock derived from the branches was ample, there were some, such as the best qualities of wines and brandies, quinine, &c., which could only be obtained by cash purchases. The transportation of their supplies, though much of it was given by railroad companies, was still very expensive, while the maintenance of their homes, lodges, offices and directories, required a heavy outlay. The Commission, as such, received no compensation, and of its officers, the President, Vice-President, and Treasurer, received no pay; while the Associate Secretary for the West, the only other member of the Commission now in service (except the Executive Committee), having left his residence and practice at Cleveland for Louisville in the Commission's service, has a moderate salary. The Commission has regarded it necessary for the proper performance of its extensive, varied, and onerous duties, to employ paid agents, and has in its employ about 200; to none of them are salaries paid so large as they could receive in other business, but they remain in the work because they love it. The aggregate of salaries is now about $15,000 per month, and of other expenses from $30,000 to $35,000 per month, making a total sum of $45,000 to $50,000 per month. The expenditure of supplies varies with the occurrence of great battles. During, and immediately after, the battles at Gettysburg, supplies to the value of $75,000 were distributed there. To the army of the Cumberland, within ten days after the disastrous battle of Chickamauga, 6,000 packages were sent; and immediately after Chattanooga, 5,000 packages and boxes went forward.

The receipts of the Commission, from its organization in June, 1861, to March, 1864, have been in money $1,133,628.28; of this amount nearly $700,000 has been received from the States and territories on the Pacific slope, including about $550,000 from California alone. Aside from this, its branches have received in money to March 1, 1864, about $650,000, which has been expended in the purchase of supplies, in local relief, and in the support of establishments of special relief under their direct charge. The value of supplies contributed cannot of course be exactly ascertained; it has, however, been estimated as carefully as possible, and considerably exceeds $7,000,000.

During the autumn and winter of 1863-4, a series of Fairs have been held in several of the principal cities of the Union, in the interest of the Commission and its branches. These fairs have been more gigantic in their conception and execution, and have yielded larger returns than any enterprises of the kind ever attempted in this country. The first of these was held at Chicago, and its development and magnificent success was due in a great measure to the energy and executive ability of Mrs. A. H. Hoge, and Mrs. D. P. Livermore, the leading spirits in the Chicago branch of the Commission, or as it is now officially known, the Northwestern Sanitary Commission. The Executive Committee visited the principal cities and large towns of Northern Illinois, Wisconsin, and Iowa, and aroused an intense enthusiasm for the work. Contributions poured in from all quarters, and as a renewed manifestation of the patriotism and loyalty of the Northwest, the Fair was worth infinitely more than it cost. The gross proceeds, when the account is completely closed, will fall but little short of $100,000, and will yield a net result of about $85,000. This branch of the Sanitary Commission has been inferior to no other in efficiency. It has furnished, from the beginning of the war to January, 1864, over $1,500,000 value of supplies, besides raising large amounts of money, which have been mostly expended in the purchase of supplies and the support of the Cairo Agency and Home for sick and wounded soldiers.

The next of these great Fairs was held in Boston, and awakened anew the enhusiasm of the people of the Old Bay State, an enthusiasm which has not materially flagged from the first moment of the war. The net receipts, thus far (the account is not yet closed), have been about $140,000. To this succeeded one at Cincinnati, which called forth the energies of the people of the Ohio Valley, and resulted in a great success not only financially but in the increase of patriotic fervor. The gross receipts were over $263,000, and the net proceeds about $240,000. Fairs for the same purpose were held soon after at Albany, at Washington, D. C., and at Yonkers, N. Y., the net proceeds of the first (the only one which has reported) were about $80,000.

On the 22d of February a Fair was opened at Brooklyn, N. Y., to which the people of Long Island generally contributed. Its gross receipts were $425,000, and the net amount realized was $400,000. The Metropolitan Fair, to commence in New York city on the 28th of March, wi.l, it is believed, eclipse in the vastness of its receipts, all of those which have preceded it, and perhaps yield an amount greater than the aggregate of the whole. It has enlisted the sympathies, the contributions, and the earnest labor of all classes. These Fairs prove conclusively that the people, so far from being wearied of the war, and tired of making sacrifices for it, are only now beginning to realize its magnitude, and to contribute in some proportion to their means, to its needs. The unanimity of sentiment which prevails among the masses as to the necessity of a vigorous prosecution of the war, to the utter overthrow of the rebellion, has been, from the first, the controlling motive in these liberal sacrifices for the soldiers.

But vast as the resources and expenditure of the United States Sanitary Commission, and much as it has done for the army, it has not acted alone in these measures of relief and solace The Western

Sanitary Commission, whose headquarters are at St. Louis, an organization wholly distinct from the one already described, has borne an honorable part in the work of providing for the wants of sick and wounded soldiers on the field, in camp, and post, and general hospitals, and on the hospital steamers, on the Mississippi, Tennessee, and Cumberland rivers. Like the United States Commission, it knows no State boundaries, but ministers alike to the soldiers who come from the East and the West, although from its location it has ministered only to the western armies. It derived its first authority to act from the following order of Major-General Fremont:

HEADQUARTERS, WESTERN DEPARTMENT,
ST. LOUIS, MO., Sept. 5, 1861.

SPECIAL ORDERS, NO. 159.

With a view to the health and comfort of the Volunteer troops in and near to the city of St. Louis, a Sanitary Commission is hereby appointed, to consist of five gentlemen, who shall serve voluntarily, and be removable at pleasure. Its general object shall be to carry out, under the properly-constituted military authorities, and in compliance with their orders, such sanitary regulations and reforms as the well-being of the soldiers demand.

The Commission shall have authority *under the directions of the Medical Director*, to select, fit up, and furnish suitable buildings for Army and Brigade Hospitals, in such place, and in such manner as circumstances require. It will attend to the selection and appointment of women nurses, under the authority and by the direction of Miss D. L. Dix, General Superintendent of the nurses of Military *Hospitals in the United States. It will* co-operate with the Surgeons of the several hospitals in providing male nurses, and in whatever manner practicable, and by their consent. It shall have authority to visit the different camps, to consult with the commanding officers, and the Colonels and other officers of the several regiments, with regard to the sanitary and general condition of the troops, and aid them in providing proper means for the preservation of health and prevention of sickness, by supplies of wholesome and well-cooked food, by good systems of drainage, and other practicable methods It will obtain from the community at large such additional means of increasing the comfort and promoting the moral and social welfare of the men, in camp and hospital, as may be needed, and cannot be furnished by Government regulations. It will, from time to time, report directly to the Commander-in-chief of the department, the condition of the camps and hospitals, with such suggestions as can properly be made by a Sanitary Board.

This Commission is not intended in any way to interfere with the Medical Staff, or other officers of the army, but to co-operate with them, and aid them in the discharge of their present arduous and extraordinary duties. It will be treated by all officers of the army, both regular and volunteer, in this Department, with the respect due to the humane and patriotic motives of the members, and to the authority of the Commander-in-chief.

This Sanitary Commission will, for the present, consist of Jas. E. Yeatman, Esq.; C. S. Greeley, Esq.; J. B. Johnson, M. D.; George Partridge, Esq.; and the Rev. William G. Eliot, D. D.

By order of Major-General JOHN C. FREMONT.

J. C. KELTON,
Assistant Adjutant-General.

The authority conferred by this order was recognized and confirmed by Major-General Halleck, who added Dr. S. Pollak to the Commission, and still later, viz., December 16, 1862, by an order from the Secretary of War (Hon. E. M.

Stanton), extending the field of its labors, and reappointing the members of the Commission as at first constituted.

This Commission has not devoted its attention to as wide a range of topics as the United States Sanitary Commission, but has confined itself to the work of superintending hospitals, furnishing supplies, appointing nurses, visiting and caring for the sick and wounded of the army of the Southwest Frontier, the District of East Arkansas, the armies operating on both sides of the Mississippi, and the Mississippi Naval Flotilla; it has at all times acted in concert with the Medical Directors and Inspectors of these armies, and on account of their efficient supervision of the condition and sanitary wants of the armies under their charge, has not found it necessary to appoint separate medical inspectors. It has the superintendence of twelve hospitals (one for officers and another for military prisoners), having accommodations for about eight thousand patients, besides ten large hospital steamers and floating hospitals; it has established Soldiers' Homes, and Soldiers' Lodges, at St. Louis, Memphis, and Columbus, Ky., and agencies at Helena, Milliken's Bend, and Springfield, Mo. and has prepared, published and distributed, a large edition of a "Treatise on the Preservation of the Health of the Soldier, the cooking of food, the preparation of diet for the sick, the duties of nurses and attendants, and the organization and general management of Hospitals." It has, during the year past, given special attention to the necessities of the freedmen in the Mississippi Valley, and its officers have interested themselves in the adjustment of wages, and in securing just and considerate treatment of the emancipated slaves from those who have rented the plantations, which had been abandoned by Rebel owners. The commission have expended about $40,000 in the relief of freedmen. It has also kept a registry of the location and condition of invalid and wounded soldiers in the Western armies.

From the commencement of the war to May 1, 1863, this Commission had received cash donations to the amount of $151,381.18, and sanitary stores and supplies of the estimated value of $395,-335.96, making a total of $546,716.14, and the expenses incurred in the collection and distribution of this large amount were only $8,848.86, or 1⅝ per cent. of the entire amount received and distributed. The amount of cash and sanitary stores received since that time, make the aggregate of its receipts, to March 1, 1864, about $1,750,000 since the war commenced. This Commission will hold at St. Louis, during the spring of the present year, a large Fair, to replenish its treasury, and its abundant and useful labors give good reason to hope that it will elicit large contributions from the patriotic citizens of the country.

CHAPTER IV.

Other Sanitary Commissions.—The Iowa State Sanitary Commission.—The Indiana State Sanitary Commission.—Similar organizations elsewhere.—The New England Soldiers' Relief Association.—State and other Relief Associations not connected with the National Organizations.—State agencies at New York, Philadelphia, Washington, Louisville, and elsewhere.—The Ladies' Aid Society of Philadelphia.—Citizens' Volunteer Hospital at Philadelphia.—The use of Hospitals donated elsewhere.—Ambulances for sick and wounded Soldiers, built and maintained by Philadelphia Firemen.—Individual Contributions to Soldiers in hospitals and on the field, not connected with any of these organizations.

Two or three of the Western States have established organizations dependent partly upon legislative grants, and partly upon contributions, for the care of the sick and wounded soldiers of their respective States, and their families, to which they have, unwisely as it seems to us, given the name of "State Sanitary Commissions." There should not be, and with most of these agencies there is not, any recognition of State lines in the distribution of supplies to the soldiers who have succumbed to disease or wounds in fighting our national battles, or serving in our national armies. They are all soldiers of our common republic, and it is a matter of no moment whether their local allegiance is due to a State on the western, northern, or eastern frontier, or in the States which constitute the heart of the body politic. There are, however, services which may be more appropriately rendered to a soldier by his own State, or its representatives, than by others; such as the furnishing means of reaching home during a furlough, or of reaching his regiment when he has been detained from it by sickness; the procuring of the allotment of his pay or bounty, or the rendering him contented by care for his family. In these, and many other ways, a State organization may do much to increase the soldier's efficiency and comfort. The Indiana State Sanitary Commission, fostered and prompted by he energetic and patriotic Governor of that State, has accomplished much good in this way, and up to February, 1864, has expended $320,000 in its succor of Indiana soldiers. The Iowa State Sanitary Commission has been also very efficient. It has expended $175,500 to February 1, 1864. An organization of a similar character, though we believe not with the same name, exists in Wisconsin, having originated with the late lamented Governor, Louis P. Harvey, who lost his life in a journey to the field of Shiloh, to distribute its bounties. It has contributed largely to the aid of the soldiers, and its benefactions have not been confined to those from Wisconsin. In Illinois, there is an officer called a Commissioner-General, whose function it is to collect stores and supplies from the towns and counties of the State and send them forward for distribution, after each great battle. In New York, a State Soldiers' Depot was established in

July, 1863, in Howard street, New York city, and received an appropriation from the State Legislature of $200,000, which combines the character of a Soldiers' Home, hospital, and reading-room, and has its couriers on each train on which New York and other soldiers come from the army of the Potomac, and meets them coming from other points, by steamers or otherwise, cares for the comfort of the sick and wounded, administering, under the direction of its surgeon, cordials and nutriment while in transit, protects them from the sharpers who would plunder them and in every way looks after their interests. It has expended since its organization in June, 1863, about $65,000 in money, and has distributed clothing, &c., to the amount of over $10,000 more. It has fed and lodged over 15,000 soldiers, and given aid and counsel to thousands more. The plan for establishing national cemeteries in the vicinity of our great battle-fields, at Gettysburg, Antietam,

Chattanooga, &c., has been greatly promoted by its earnest advocacy.

One of the best, as it is really one of the most national, of the institutions of this class, is "The New England Soldiers' Relief Association," located at 194 Broadway, New York, and organized April 3, 1862. Its founders and supporters were New England men and women, but its doors have been opened to, and its charities lavished upon, the soldiers of every State. That a soldier was on furlough, or sick or wounded, discharged, or in trouble, has been ever a sufficient passport to its halls, and its sympathies. Since its organization, it has received, registered, lodged, fed, aided, and clothed sick and wounded or disabled soldiers from thirty-one States, the District of Columbia, the regular army, the navy, and the Invalid Corps, to the number of about 45,000, and has fed or lodged, and rendered assistance to many thousands more, who were not sick, wounded, or disabled. It has a Hospital Record and Directory, very full and complete, of the inmates of all the military hospitals of New York and New England, which is kept up to date by daily reports from each hospital, and gives full particulars in regard to the location, condition, and final disposition of each patient. This register contains about 40,000 names, and is so complete that the Sanitary Commission, in February, 1864, relinquished theirs for that Department, in its favor. It has an excellent hospital for the sick or wounded soldier, with a skillful surgeon, careful attendants, and assiduous volunteer night watchers; furnishes an asylum to those unfortunate soldiers who, discharged from the service without means, find themselves homeless and shelterless, giving them a home till employment can be provided for them. It also interests itself in procuring transportation, bounties, and back pay for the soldiers, and furnishing information to the friends of those who are sick, or have died, relative to procuring their dues. Religious services are conducted every Sabbath at its rooms. Since August, 1863, it has had two couriers at the expense of the State of Massachusetts, running between New York and Washington, and caring for all soldiers in the cars. The work of the Association has been conducted with a very small money expenditure, only about $28,000 in cash having been received by its Treasurer. It has, however, received very considerable amounts of supplies of clothing, food, delicacies for the sick, &c., &c., probably to a value not less than $200,000. It could, however, make a good use of a much larger amount. Much of the service rendered, including that of the Superintendent, is voluntary, and without compensation. Indeed, the Superintendent has, in addition, paid large sums from his own pocket, for the relief of soldiers, in cases where such relief could not properly come from the State funds, or the funds of the Association. Colonel F. E. Howe, the Superintendent of this Association, acts also in the capacity of State Military Agent for the States of Maine, New Hampshire, Vermont, Massachusetts, Wisconsin, Minnesota, and Indiana, and is authorized to render such assistance as may be needed to the soldiers of those States coming to New York.

Most of the other loyal States have military agents at New York, and some of them at Philadelphia. At Washington, each of the loyal States, east of the Rocky Mountains, has a representative body, composed of citizens of those States, resident temporarily or permanently at the capital. Members of Congress, &c., who interest themselves in the welfare of the soldiers of their respective States, raise money among themselves, and collect supplies from their States, which are distributed in the hospitals around Washington, or in many cases sent to the front, before, during, or after a battle. The Sanitary Commission has now become the almoner of some of these organizations, as from its peculiar facilities it might well do with all of them ; but prior to July, 1863, they had distributed in money and stores, the amount, as estimated, of $1,030,000. There have been also similar State agencies connected with most of the Western States, at Louisville, Nashville, St. Louis, &c.

There have been a few Ladies' Aid Societies which have not affiliated themselves with either the United States Sanitary Commission or its branches, or the Western Sanitary Commission, preferring, for some reason, independent action. Prominent among them is the Ladies' Aid Society of Philadelphia, an association organized on the 26th of April, 1861, and which has labored assiduously from that time to the present, promoting by every means in its power the physical and moral welfare of the soldier. It has a number of auxiliaries in the State, and has had its efficient Secretary, Mrs. John Harris, in the field and ministering in person to the wants of the sick and suffering soldiers, with, for the most part, two or three assistants, since the first battles on the Peninsula in the spring of 1862. It had expended in money, to November 1, 1863, $19,380, and had sent from the Philadelphia office, food, clothing, &c., to the value of over $60,000, besides other supplies sent direct from various points to Mrs. Harris, to an aggregate amount of probably not far from $200,000. The Soldiers' Aid Society of Hartford, Connecticut, has been another association which has acted independently, and has expended about $20,000 in money and over $50,000 in supplies. In most of the larger cities there have been associations of a similar character, which have either distributed their food, clothing, &c., by special, and usually unpaid agents, or have forwarded them to some of the State organizations—at Washington, Louisville, &c., or have consigned them to individuals engaged in this work in the army, or at prominent points. The aggregate amount of such contributions is large, though composed of a thousand little rills. The aggregate sent to Washington and its vicinity, including Baltimore, up to July, 1863, was ascertained by careful inquiry to be somewhat more than $1,350,000, and to Cincinnati, St. Louis, Louisville, Cairo, Nashville, Memphis and New Orleans, to not less than $1,500,000.

The amount of supplies of delicacies, extra food, cordials, clothing, and bedding furnished to temporary and permanent military hospitals, aside from those furnished by the Sanitary Commissions, has been very large. In the summer and autumn of 1862, the civil hospitals of the northern cities were filled to overflowing with the sick and wounded, and numerous churches, barracks, and other buildings were temporarily used for hospital purposes, and the resources of the Medical and Quartermaster's Bureaux were completely drained in supplying hospital clothing and furniture, and ordinary provisions and medicines, long before the half were fully supplied. Contributions poured in freely from the people of what was needed, and kitchens were established in connection with most of the hospitals, in which ladies of the highest social position, in their turns, served and prepared the delicacies which would be most grateful to the sick. Papers, periodicals, books, stationery and postage were furnished in liberal quantities to the convalescent, and letters written to the friends of the patients by these volunteer nurses. After the Government had established its own permanent hospitals (though a considerable number of them were hospital buildings furnished rent free by cities or towns) the same course was pursued in most of them, but in a considerable number the supplies were furnished by the

Sanitary Commission. The value of these supplies furnished by private hands to several of these hospitals, in New York, Philadelphia, and Washington, has been carefully ascertained, and averaging the expenditure as proportioned to the inmates of most of the hospitals of the period (some fared better and few worse) the contributions for this purpose could not have been less in value than $2,200,000.

One of these hospitals, now under the charge of the Government, originated in the philanthropic spirit of the citizens of that portion of Philadelphia residing in the vicinity of the Baltimore station-house, in Broad street. After the great battles before Washington, in the summer of 1862, trains, freighted with the wounded, poured into Philadelphia, and no provisions having been made for their quiet and speedy transfer to the hospitals, most of which were at considerable distance, they were temporarily placed in churches, or the station-house, often greatly to their discomfort, and sometimes with a fatal result. The citizens of the vicinity, a large portion of them mechanics, laboring by day in the busy manufactories of that vicinity, were greatly distressed at witnessing this suffering, and resolved, though with but very small available means, to erect near the station-house a hospital for the temporary accommodation of sick and wounded soldiers. A landholder generously gave them the use of some vacant lots on the corner of Broad and Prince streets; others contributed lumber, furniture, heating apparatus, bath-tubs, and some, money. One poor Irishman wheeled a half-worn stove to the new hospital. "He had nothing else to give," he said, "and must do something for the sogers." The hospital was erected, and furnished with five hundred beds in fifteen days, at a cost of over $9,000. It was subsequently enlarged, so as to give accommodations for seven hundred beds, and has, in addition, two kitchens, bath-rooms, and a large dining-room. It has received over 2,500 patients in a day, and has lodged more than 700 at night. Nearly 40,000 soldiers have been admitted since it was opened. It has received, in money, about $23,300 to March 1, 1864, and expended about $20,000. It has received also in clothing, food, liquors, and delicacies, not less than $30,000.

The feeling of sympathy and patriotism which has actuated the masses of the people, manifested itself in numberless instances of thoughtfulness and tenderness, even from classes, among whom it was hardly to be looked for. A memorable example of this occurred in Philadelphia, where, when the wounded were brought to the city, and carried, not perhaps so gently as they might have been, in hired conveyances, to the hospitals, the firemen said to each other: "These poor fellows deserve tenderer care and handling than they will receive from hired hackmen; we will build ambulances for them, and carry them to the hospitals ourselves." To this thoughtfulness it is owing that there are now twenty-six of these ambulances, luxurious affairs, costing from $500 to $800 each, drawn by two horses, and kept always ready in the engine houses of the fire companies for the transportation of sick and wounded, and that in these they are carried, attended by firemen, and handled as gently as a mother would handle her infant, to the hospitals, and without any compensation.

The individual contributions to the benefit of the soldiers and their families, not coming into the treasury of any organization, were in the aggregate of vast amount; how vast can never be known, even with approximate accuracy, but that they must have risen to millions of money or money value, is past question. At the commencement of the war, when great numbers of clerks and mechanics enlisted for three months in the militia regiments, their employers, with very few exceptions, voluntarily offered to pay, and did pay, their salaries during their absence, and restored them to their positions on their return. The same thing occurred, though not to quite the same extent, in the summer of 1862 and 1863, in both which seasons the militia of New York, Brooklyn, Philadelphia, and other cities were called out. One of the wealthiest citizens of New York, Cornelius Vanderbilt, Esq., presented to the Government his magnificent steamship the "Vanderbilt," which had cost him over a million of dollars, and was at that time worth in cash, $800,000. Several of the great express lines offered to carry goods intended for the soldiers, free; others reduced their prices on such goods one-half, and throughout the war, sanitary stores and the agents and delegates of the Sanitary and Christian Commissions have been very generally, we might almost say universally, carried free over the principal railroads of the country, and the messages of both have been borne on the telegraph lines without charge.

The supplying of the wants of the families of the soldiers, has been to a large extent a work of private beneficence, and has involved the payment of much larger sums than many suppose. So, too, the sending or giving to the soldiers small sums for the purchase of luxuries, tobacco, and the like, has in the aggregate amounted to hundreds of thousands of dollars.

The establishment of soldiers' asylums or homes, by several of the States, or as has been the case in most instances, by voluntary contribution under a State charter, institutions where the maimed or crippled soldier, who is without a home, may find comfort and light employment when he desires it, is another of the manifestations of the interest which the nation feels in its soldiers. The same spirit is exhibited, though in a somewhat sadder way, in the establishment of orphan asylums for the children of soldiers deceased in the war, and of homes for soldiers' widows ; the provision made in many of our literary institutions for the free education of soldiers' sons and daughters, and the readiness with which employment is furnished to a disabled soldier in any capacity which he can fill. Very often, too, it is seen in the shy, respectful, but diffident way in which, as fearful of giving pain, money is slipped into the hand of the maimed, wounded, or crippled soldier. not to encourage or sanction mendicity, but in love for the cause to which he has sacrificed a limb or suffered a wound, There is almost universally among our people, a feeling of reverence for the battle-scarred and wounded soldier, as for one who, standing face to face with death in the struggle for our country's life, has only come off victor by fearful struggle and terrible suffering. God grant that naught in the future may abate this reverential love.

CHAPTER V.

THE NECESSITY FOR MORAL AND RELIGIOUS INSTRUCTION AND CONSOLATION IN THE ARMY.—THE EFFORTS OF THE YOUNG MENS' CHRISTIAN ASSOCIATIONS.—THE ORGANIZATION OF THE UNITED STATES CHRISTIAN COMMISSION.—ITS PURPOSES.—THE IMPORTANCE OF COMBINING PHYSICAL RELIEF WITH SPIRITUAL TEACHING.—THE LABORS OF THE CHRISTIAN COMMISSION.—WHAT IT HAS ACCOMPLISHED.—OTHER INSTITUTIONS FOR SUPPLYING THE MORAL AND RELIGIOUS WANTS OF THE ARMY.—BIBLE SOCIETIES.—TRACT SOCIETIES.—PUBLICATION SOCIETIES.—MISSIONARY SOCIETIES.—INDIVIDUAL EFFORTS.

WHILE the Sanitary Commission and the numerous other societies and associations were doing what they could for the improvement of the physical condition of the soldier, the maintenance of his health, and his restoration from sickness, acquired in a malarious climate, the repairing of war's fearful ravages, and the soothing of the pangs of dissolution, there was a strong and growing feeling in the minds of the religious public, that these ends and aims, though good, and by no means to be neglected, were not all which the condition of our army demanded.

The soldier has a soul as well as a body, a soul to be blighted and polluted by the vices of the camp, or to be kept pure and holy for that change of worlds which to so many must come with fearful suddenness. It was needed that the Christian influences, from which so many had gone forth to the camp and battle-field, should not be replaced by intoxication, blasphemy, and obscenity; that the obscene book and the pack of cards should not take the place of the Scriptures, the Christian narrative, or the religious newspaper; that the Sabbath should not be desecrated beyond what the exigencies of the service demanded. They would have the Gospel, with its benign influences, follow the soldier into the camp; they would stimulate his courage by giving it a higher and holier basis; animate his patriotism by making Christianity its foundation, and enliven his faith in the future triumph of his cause, by showing him that it was the cause of God. For the sick and wounded they would invoke healing mercies for both soul and body from the Great Physician, and point them, in the struggle with the last enemy, to Him who is the Abolisher of Death, the Conqueror of the Grave.

It was in consequence of these convictions that, from the commencement of the war, the Young Men's Christian Assiciations, in most of the larger cities and towns of the loyal States, had contributed largely, not only in money and supplies, to the relief and comfort of the soldiers, but in personal service. Many of their members were in the army, and the sympathy felt for them by those who remained at home prompted to efficient action for the spiritual as well as physical needs of the army. After every considerable battle, members of these associations were dispatched with money, sanitary stores and supplies, and religious and moral reading matter, for free distribution to the sufferers. One Young Men's Christian Association, that of Brooklyn, N. Y., had contributed in this way more than $28,000 for this purpose, and had given in addition the voluntary services of several of its members in distributing supplies and caring for the sick and wounded on the battle-fields of the East and the West. Others had done nearly as much, some, perhaps, even more.

At a convention of these Christian Associations, held in New York, November 16, 1861, it was resolved to organize from the representatives of these bodies a United States Christian Commission, and the following persons were appointed: Rev. Rollin H. Neale, D. D., Boston; George H. Stuart, Esq., Philadelphia; Rev. Bishop E. S. Janes, D. D., New York; Rev. M. L. R. P. Thompson, D. D., Cincinnati; Hon. Benjamin F. Manierre, New York; Colonel Clinton B. Fisk, St. Louis; Rev. Benjamin C. Cutler,

D. D., Brooklyn ; John V. Farwell, Esq., Chicago ; Mitchell H. Miller, Esq., Washington; John D. Hill, M. D., Buffalo. During the succeeding year Mr. Manierre and Rev. Dr. Cutler resigned, and their places were filled by the appointment of Jay Cooke, Esq., of Philadelphia, and Rev. James Eells, D.D., of Brooklyn.

Soon after its appointment the Commission met in Washington, and organized by choosing George H. Stuart, of Philadelphia, Chairman, and B. F. Manierre, of New York, Secretary and Treasurer. Its headquarters were at first established in New York, and Rev. A. M. Morrison was appointed Secretary, when it was ascertained that the labors of the two offices would be too much for one man. Mr. Morrison's services were rendered gratuitously. Some months were occupied in the organization of branches, in obtaining from Government and from railroad and telegraph lines, passes, and in adjusting the details for the vast work which soon began to flow in upon them, and it was not till the summer of 1862, that the Commission was fairly ready for its work; meantime its headquarters had been removed to Philadelphia, and Rev. William E. Boardman appointed Secretary in place of Rev. Mr. Morrison, resigned.

Its objects, as declared in its circulars, were "to arouse the Christian Associations and the Christian men and women of the loyal States to such action toward the men in our army and navy as would be pleasing to the Master; to obtain and direct volunteer labors, and to collect stores and money with which to supply whatever is needed, reading matter and articles necessary for health, not furnished by Government or other agencies, and to give the officers and men of our army and navy the best Christian ministries, for both body and soul, possible in their circumstances."

The Commission is organized upon the

principle of voluntary, unpaid agency. Its Chairman, a merchant of Philadelphia, not only devotes almost his entire time to its service, but furnishes office-room and storage, clerks, porters, &c., to conduct the business correspondence and pack the stores and supplies, free of charge. The railroad companies have uniformly given free passes to its delegates, and the telegraph companies free transmission to its messages. It has been largely aided by grants of Bibles, religious books, tracts, &c., from the Bible and publishing societies, and donations of newspapers, religious and secular, from the publishers of those papers ; its delegates are volunteers, whose expenses of living are alone furnished by the Commission, and who spend some weeks or months in ministrations of kindness to the sick and wounded ; it has also employed a very large corps of volunteer chaplains to visit the regiments and brigades of the army, and manifest their sympathy with the soldier, and seek to improve his physical and moral condition.

While thus a voluntary system, it acts only under the sanction and with the approval of the Government and its officers. The surgeons and chaplains of the army are among its best friends. Understanding fully that there is sometimes "more gospel in a loaf of bread than in a sermon," it bestows the loaf of bread where it is needed, and the Gospel also. Its distribution of its stores of food, clothing, medicines, &c., are made with the approval and consent of the proper officers only, and have amounted to somewhat more than half a million of dollars in value, in the two years since its organization. During that period it has commissioned 1,563 Christian ministers and laymen to minister to men on battlefields, in camps, hospitals, and ships ; has distributed 568,275 copies of the Scriptures, 502,556 copies of hymn and psalm books, 1,410,061 other books, 155,145 pamphlets, 3,326,250 religious newspapers, and 22,930,428 pages of tracts. It has received over $400,000 in money, and over $700,000 in stores, books, and donations of other descriptions. During the winter, it has aided the regiments in camps to erect temporary chapels, of logs with canvas roofs, in which they have held religious meetings with beneficial effects.

Other religious organizations have incurred large expenditures in the promotion of the spiritual welfare of the national army and navy. The American Bible Society has donated Bibles and Testaments, either directly or through its auxiliaries, to the amount of about $300,000; and about one-sixth of this amount has been in grants to the rebels, the Bibles and Testaments, having, by permission of the United States Government, been sent by flag of truce to the rebel lines and received there by their officers.

The American Tract Society, New York, entered very heartily, and very early, into the work of supplying their books, tracts, and papers to the army and navy, and found them readily received, and eagerly read by the soldiers and sailors. They state that nearly every regiment in the Union army has received more or less of their publications; they have been supplied from the General Depository of the Society, and its agencies at commercial cities, and at camps, recruiting stations, and hospitals, in all the Western, Middle, and Northern States, and at camps and hospitals in front, in the different departments of the army. The secretaries and agents of the Society have made frequent visits to different divisions of the army, and army missionaries have traversed the camps in their faithful visitations. Libraries have been established in the hospitals; hundreds of ships of war and gunboats have been supplied when fitting out, and their chaplains, pious officers or sailors, are supplied from month to month. As a result, it may be said that there is scarcely a camp upon the field, or regiment in the ranks, or ward in the hospital, or mess in the navy, where the publications of this Society have not been distributed, or where they do not find a welcome reception. Since the war commenced, the Society has issued more than 300 distinct publications, with special reference to the supply of the army and navy, and the freedmen. Of these, there have been printed and bound 1,217,000 volumes, 2,735,096 tracts, and 649,000 cards and hand-bills, making a total of 4,602,096 publications, nearly all of which have been distributed in the army and navy. Besides these, there have also been circulated in the same quarters, many thousand copies of "The Child's Paper," and more than a million copies of the "American Messenger," in English and German. This distribution, and the army work of the Society, including the labors of agents, colporteurs, and army missionaries, visiting the encampments and hospitals in the different departments, have cost the Society about $100,000.

Not less active and earnest has been the American Tract Society, at Boston, one of whose Secretaries has devoted himself wholly to the work of visiting the army and superintending the distribution among the camps of the East the publications of that Society, while its efficient Western Secretary has performed a similar work in the armies of the West. Both gentlemen have exerted themselves also in personal ministrations to the sick and wounded soldiers. This Society has published a large number of different works with special reference to the wants of the army and navy, and of these has issued: Of bound volumes, 527,000; of tracts, 2,358,400; of papers, 231,232; or a total of publications of 3,116,632. They have also sent a large number of these books and tracts, of a more general character, to the hospital and other libraries, &c., but of these they have no exact account. The expenditure of the Society in its army and navy work, to March 1, 1864, has been $70,229.85. The American Sunday-School Union, the Christian Alliance, the Presbyterian Board of Publication, the Presbyterian (N. S.) Publication Committee, the American and Foreign Bible Society, the American Baptist Publication Society, the Episcopal Tract and Prayer Book Society, and the Reformed Dutch Board of Publication, have also each expended very considerable sums in the circulation of their publications in the army. The publishers of religious and literary periodicals and newspapers have also contributed, aside from those sent through the Christian Commission, large quantities of their papers and periodicals to the army, many of them having a small fund set apart for this purpose. The aggregate value of these publications and papers, exclusive of those of the Tract Societies, is not far from $125,000. Several of the Missionary Societies have also sent their missionaries to labor for the spiritual good of the army, and have met with encouraging success in these efforts. Of the expenditures incurred in these movements we have been unable to obtain any information. The Societies which have taken a part in this work are the American Home Missionary Society, the American Missionary Association, the American Baptist Home Mission Society, and the Free Mission Society, and perhaps some others. There were not wanting, too, instances of individual laborers, self-supported messengers of good to the soldier, who sought, without thought of pecuniary reward or profit, to promote his spiritual interests.

CHAPTER VI.

PERSONAL SERVICES IN THE AID SOCIETIES, IN THE HOSPITALS, AND IN THE FIELD.—THE SERVICES RENDERED IN THIS WAY THROUGH THE SANITARY COMMISSION.—SERVICES OF DELEGATES OF THE CHRISTIAN COMMISSION.—VOLUNTARY INDEPENDENT SERVICES OF CLERGYMEN, PHYSICIANS, AND OTHERS.—WOMAN'S LABORS IN THE WAR.—INCIDENTS.

WE have thus far spoken mainly of the philanthropy evoked by the war in its pecuniary aspects, as so much money or money's worth contributed to some one or other of its many modes of relief; but there is a philanthropy, a love of our fellow-man, of a far higher character than this, and leading to nobler and greater sacrifices than those of gold or silver, or perishable goods. These are all good and indispensable to the accomplishment of the great purposes desired; but, by the side of the spirit of self-sacrifice, the gift of personal service, the devotion of an earnest and generous nature to the work, how poor and worthless do they seem!

In this regard, also, the philanthropy of our country has not been wanting. History records with admiration the heroic spirit of self-sacrifice of the Grecian mother who sent forth her only son to the battle-field with a shield bearing the device, "Return with this, or upon it." In yet higher colors does it paint the fearless spirit of the women of Carthage, who, by the side of their fathers, brothers, lovers, and sons, endured cheerfully the horrors of the Roman siege, and when suffering the tortures of incipient starvation, cut from their heads their beautiful tresses, to furnish bowstrings to their brave defenders. To our own time, and our loftier, riper civilization, has it been given to make greater and more glorious sacrifices than these, to hallow its offerings upon the altar of our country, by moistening them with the heart's best blood ; to give the best powers of highly gifted natures to the ministrations of a patriotic tenderness, and not unseldom to lay down, in these ministrations, lives of priceless value and of angelic purity.

The war has not been conducted with hireling troops, mercenary wretches, procured at so much per head, and only fit to be food for powder. No! each State has given to the service the purest, gentlest, noblest blood which flowed in the veins of its sons; its men of high culture, genial nature, and lofty aspiration; clergymen deeply versed in theologic lore, but yet more deeply familiar with the human heart, and its joys and sorrows; lawyers, whose eloquence thrilled all hearts, as their legal attainments and acumen had won for them high renown; physicians, whose skill and scientific knowledge made them the leaders of their profession; professors, who, leaving the universities whose chairs they had filled so well, assumed, with the utmost cheerfulness, subordinate positions, where they had been accustomed to command; statesmen, whose words of fire had echoed from the Atlantic to the Pacific, and caused a nation's heart to quiver with patriotic emotion. Promptly and joyfully they offered themselves to the work of defending their country, not always, perhaps not in a majority of cases, in positions of command, for hundreds of such men have been found as privates in the ranks.

One of the Rhode Island regiments was almost wholly composed of the most eminent citizens of that little commonwealth, and numbered a half hundred of college graduates, many of them eminent as professional men, in the ranks of its privates. A Vermont regiment numbered two score men of collegiate education among its private soldiers. An Illinois regiment (the famous Normal Regiment) was made up almost exclusively of teachers. Massachusetts sent her noblest sons to the war, in all grades of rank, and ofttimes received them back, "dead on the field of honor." The names of her Webster, Willard, Wilson, Putnam, Stearns, Stevens, Fuller, Manross, and Shaw, with those of many others, fallen on the field of battle, shall be held in everlasting remembrance. Nor they alone. Every State mourns, but with a lofty pride, its gallant dead; and the hearts of kindred, torn by the sudden and terrible stroke, yet cherish with a fonder and holier love the banner under which they fought and died.

Often, those who have been thus bereft, have themselves proved the most earnest and efficient ministrants to the sick, the suffering, and the wounded; distilling from their own wounded and sorrow-stricken hearts the balm of consolation to those who had been called to suffer for their country, and assuaging their own grief by imparting consolation to others. Some of the tenderest nurses of the hospital, or the wounded on the field, have been those on whose souls lay the shadow of a great affliction; who had come perhaps at first to minister to their own loved ones, but finding them past all need of earthly solace, have turned to those who might yet be saved to serve their country, and to defend its institutions, and with a sad but loving zeal, sought their restoration to health.

There have been few instances in history of a more sublime devotion to a great and good object than have been exhibited by some of the officers of the Sanitary Commission. For a period of almost three years, its President has given, without fee or reward, to its service, the best hours of every day, and has borne its great and varied duties, and the measures for the best development of its rapidly increasing powers of usefulness, upon his heart—a work sufficient to task to the utmost the powers of any man, whatever his business capacities. The members of the Executive Committee of the Commission, all men whose professional or business position made large demands upon their time, have hardly fallen short of their President in their arduous labors. The medical members of the Commission, occupying the very highest rank in the profession, have given much time, thought, and labor, to its duties; and the Special Medical Inspectors, men who have a world wide reputation, in their arduous round of visiting the Military Hospitals, have conferred a benefit on the nation, for which money could not compensate. The regular Medical Inspectors, too, as well as the volunteer assistants on hospital transports, in camp hospitals, and on the battle-field, have given themselves to the work with an earnestness and zeal which money could not buy, and, in too many instances, have sacrificed their lives to the intensity of their labors of mercy. The General Secretary and Associate Secretaries have not been wanting in ability, energy, and patriotism, and the promptness and harmony with which all their plans are executed speak well for the spirit which pervades them.

The officers of the Western Sanitary Commission, and of the Christian Commission, and the delegates of the latter, whether clerical or lay, have shown all the ardor and zeal of volunteers, together with the capacity for quiet, steady, protracted hard work, often under very trying circumstances, which indicates the true character of their patriotism.

In other organizations, or working independently, but with a full appreciation of their relative duties to the Soldier and the Government, there are many men who have won for themselves the undying remembrance of the soldier, and of Him who said, "Inasmuch as ye did it unto one of the least of these my brethren, ye did it unto me."

This patriotic impulse to render aid and comfort to our soldiers at any sacrifice of time or service, has been especially manifest on the occasion of great battles.

Immediately after the battle of Shiloh, and again after Antietam, and Fredericksburg, Stone River, Gettysburg, Vicksburg, and Chickamauga, physicians and surgeons, the most eminent in their profession, volunteered by scores to go to the battle-field, or the temporary hospital, and exerted their best skill for the care and healing of the country's defenders. Clergymen, pastors of large and wealthy congregations, sought the opportunity of ministering to the sick and dying soldier, of breathing into the ear, fast growing dull to earthly sounds, the words of spiritual consolation, and of receiving from lips soon to become silent in death, utterances of faith and messages of love. Senators and Representatives in Congress; Judges of the highest Courts, and members of the bar, of the most brilliant reputation, sought, in ministrations to these wounded and dying heroes, to taste the luxury of doing good. Among those not connected with the learned professions, too, there was the same earnestness and self-sacrifice.

In more than one instance, men brought up in luxury, with all the advantages of high and generous culture and foreign travel, but who, ennuyéd by a life without an object, had been almost ready to regard existence as a burden, have found in the work of alleviating the sufferings of the soldier their true vocation, and have given to it their best energies, realizing in their heightened enjoyment, that

> "The act of mercy is twice blessed ;
> It blesses him that gives and him that takes."

In this work of holy philanthropy, however, woman has borne the most glorious part. Here as ever, in sorrow and anguish, as a ministering angel, she has done her holiest work, and won her brightest trophies. Could the sacrifices, the self-denials, the persistent, wearing labor, and the moral heroism of the women of this country, during the past three years, be fully recorded, the narrative would be without a parallel in the annals of history, for its thrilling interest, its deep pathos, and its sublime courage. But while such a record can only be made by Him who knows the secrets of all hearts, there are occasional glimpses afforded to us, which show the spirit which has actuated so many of them. It is not by any means the educated and gifted alone who have been the heroines of this period, if utter self-abnegation, and a devotion which rises above all else to comprehend alone the ideas of God and our country, constitute heroism. In that little hamlet on the bleak and barren hills of New England, far away from the great city, or even the populous village, you will find a mother and daughter living in a humble dwelling. The husband and father has lain for many years 'neath the sod in the graveyard on the hill slope; the only son, the hope and joy of both mother and sister, at the call of duty, gave himself to the service of his country, and left those whom he loved as his own life to toil at home alone. By and by, at Williamsburg, or Fair Oaks, or in that terrible retreat to James River, or at Cedar Mountain, it matters not which, the swift speeding bullet laid him low, and after days, or it may be weeks, of terrible suffering, he gave up his young life on the altar of his country. The shock was a terrible one to those lone dwellers on the snowy hills. He was their all; but it was for the cause of Freedom, of Right, of God; and hushing the wild beating of their hearts, they bestir themselves, in their deep poverty, to do something for the cause for which their young hero has given his life. It is but little, for they are *sorely straitened;* but the mother, though her heart is wrapped in the darkness of sorrow, saves the expense of mourning apparel, and the daughter turns her faded dress; the little earnings of both are carefully hoarded, the pretty chintz curtains which had made their humble room cheerful are replaced by paper, and by dint of constant saving, enough money is raised to purchase the other materials for a hospital quilt, a pair of socks, and a shirt to be sent to the Relief Association, to give comfort to some poor wounded soldier tossing in agony in some distant hospital. Surely, He who noticed the widow's two mites which made a farthing, will record in His Book such deeds of love as these.

Take another case, as reported by one of the Ladies' Aid Societies. In one of the mountainous counties at the North, in a scattered farming district, lived a mother and daughters, too poor to obtain by purchase the material for making hospital clothing, yet resolved to do something for the soldier. Twelve miles distant, over the mountain, and accessible only by a road almost impassable, was the county town, in which there was a Relief Association. Borrowing a neighbor's horse, either the mother or daughters came regularly every fortnight, to procure from this society garments to make up for the hospital. They had no money; but though the care of their few acres of sterile land devolved upon them alone, they could and would find time to work for the sufferers in the hospitals. At length, curious to know the secret of such fervor in the cause, one of the Managers of the Association addressed them: "You have some relative, a son, or brother, or father, in the war, I suppose?" "No!" was the reply, "not now; our only brother fell at Ball's Bluff." "Why, then," asked the Manager, "do you feel so deep an interest in this work?" "Our country's cause is the cause of God, and we would do what we can, for His sake," was the sublime reply.

Or take yet again this incident of the Great Northwestern Sanitary Fair, related by Rev. F. N. Knapp: "Among the wagons which had drawn up near the rooms of the Sanitary Commission to unload their stores, was one peculiar for its exceeding look of poverty; it was worn and mended, and was originally made merely of poles. It was drawn by three horses, which had seen much of life, but little grain. The driver was a man past middle age, with the clothes and look of one who toiled hard, but he had a thoughtful and kindly face. He sat there quietly waiting his turn to unload. By his side, with feet over the front of the wagon, for it was filled very full, was his wife, a silent, worn-looking woman; near the rear of the wagon was a girl of fifteen, perhaps, and her sister, dressed in black, carrying in her arms a little child. Some one said to the man (after asking the woman with the child if she would not go into the Commission Rooms and get warm), 'My friend, you seem to have quite a load, here, of vegetables. Now I am curious to know what good things you are bringing the soldiers; will you tell me what you have?' 'Yes,' said he; 'here are potatoes, and here are three bags of onions, and there are some rutabaga, and there a few turnips, and that is a small bag of meal, and you can see the cabbages fill in; and that box with slats has some ducks in it, which one of them brought in.' 'Oh, then, this isn't all your load alone, is it?' 'Why, no! Our region, just where I live, is rather a hard soil, and we haven't any of us much to spare, any way; yet for this business we could have raked up as much again as this is, if we had had time. But we didn't get the notice that the wagons were going in, till last night about eight o'clock, and it was dark and raining—so I and my wife and the girls could only go round to five or six of the neighbors, within a mile or so; but we did the best we could. We worked pretty much all the night, and loaded, so as to be able to get out to the main road and start with the rest of them this morning. But I can't help it, if it is little; its *something* for those soldiers.' 'Have you a son in the army?' 'No,' he answered, slowly, after turning round and looking at his wife. 'No, I haven't, *now*, but we had one there once; he's buried down by Stone River; he was shot there. And that isn't just so, either. We called him our boy, but he was only our adopted son; we took him when he was little, so he was just the same as our boy, and' (pointing over his shoulder, without looking back) 'that's his wife, there, with the baby. But I shouldn't bring these things any quicker if he were alive now, and in the army. I don't know that I should think so much as I do now about the boys away off there.'"

In none of these cases, nor in the thousands of others of which they are but the representatives, could the desire for applause or fame have had any part in this earnest devotion to the cause of their country; there was no room for that; but the toil, hard, wearing toil, unmitigated by aught of poetry or romance, was one of the noble expressions of a self-sacrificing philanthropy.

Among those who deserve a high place on the roll of Christian philanthropists are the hundreds of noble women, who, for the space of three years past, have toiled on regularly, week after week, going to their work at the rooms of the Ladies' Aid Societies, or to their self-imposed labors at the hospitals or Homes for Soldiers, as regularly as the merchant or banker goes to his business, and sacrificing to it the enjoyments of luxurious homes more cheerfully than if it were a festive gathering. To say that they have done this work of Christian love as a duty, is a phrase too cold; they have deemed it a privilege, a matter of rejoicing, thus to make sacrifices for their country.

Nor would our record approach completeness did we fail to give due honor to those gifted women, who, delicately trained and nurtured, have gone from all the allurements of home, the enjoyments of society, the endearments of friends, to minister personally to the fevered and the maimed, in the crowded hospital, in the camp, or amid the horrors of the battle-field. We have not the space, nor is it consonant with the purpose of this work, to give the names of the scores of these heroines, but we can briefly indicate their abundant labors.*

They have, many of them, been members of families of the highest social position in the Northern States, refined, cultivated, winning, and womanly; and have left homes where they were tenderly cherished, and surrounded by every

---

* It is gratifying to learn, as we do from a recently published announcement, that a biographical record of the deeds of most of these "Heroines of the Civil War" is in preparation by a thoroughly competent writer, and is to be published soon by Mr. N. C. Miller, of New York.

luxury; and for months, and sometimes for years, have encountered the inconveniences of hospital life, or the still greater discomforts of life in the camp, an ambulance or a tent their home by day or by night, and the soldiers' ration, often scanty and sometimes unpalatable, their only fare—to "dress the sores, bind up the wounds, cheer the spirits, and medicine the maladies of those whom sickness and battle have stricken." "Why," it is often asked, "should these women, thus richly endowed, have gone forth to this work, when others, perhaps, equally competent, have remained at home in ease and comfort?" "Because," we answer, "the love of country and of our glorious institutions burned so fiercely in their hearts, that they must act; the necessity to do something for those who were doing so much for their country's preservation, was like a fire in their bones; they could not rest." To many of them, too, there came the conviction that this struggle was intimately connected with that high and peculiar civilization whose crowning glory it has been to elevate Woman. The success of the rebellion, they felt, was the triumph of barbarism; its result would be to deprive the sex of the opportunity for free and full development, intellectual and moral, and for a constant and beneficent use of all those admirable powers which God has given to woman. It was then, also, in behalf of their sex, whose social, intellectual, and moral position was imperiled by the triumph of the slaveholding power, and would be degraded by its despotism, if it were successful, that these noble women have done their utmost to succor and encourage their fathers, brothers, sons, or lovers, in the defense of a nation's honor, and a nation's liberties. Gloriously have they acquitted themselves in this work. Amid almost superhuman labors and fatigues, amid perils by water and by land, in temporary hospitals, where the enemy's shot and shell came hurtling through the walls, and now and then killed some wounded and helpless patient; in the rear on battle-fields where the heavy missiles from rifled cannon ploughed deep furrows around them; on burning sands, amid the fierce blaze of the summer's sun, at Morris Island, or on the gulf coast, or tossing upon the stormy Atlantic in hospital ships, they have never faltered; and in more than one instance have maintained their position and continued their ministry when the surgeons have fled in terror, and the army itself had commenced a disorderly retreat. The work accomplished by some of these women on the hospital transports, in the waters that bound the Peninsula, in the summer of 1862, was sublimer in its heroism and self-sacrifice than any battle of the war, and was yet more beautiful for the spirit of cheerfulness and alacrity in which it was performed. Not less sublime was the devotion which was manifested at Shiloh, at Harrison's Landing, at Antietam, at

Fredericksburg, at Stone River, and at Gettysburg. It is no matter of wonder that the soldiers have given to so many of these women the name of "angel," nor that a rough but large hearted soldier, lying in one of the hospitals of St. Louis, should have said to the gentle nurse who had so tenderly soothed his pain, "When you get to the gate of heaven, they won't ask you for a countersign; they'll let you right in!"

Several of these heroines are the widows of Generals slain in the service, who, having themselves tasted the bitter cup of anguish, delight to allay as far as possible the suffering of others; one is the widow of a patriotic Governor of one of the Western States, who lost his life in the attempt to bring relief to the wounded after the battle of Shiloh; others have lost sons or brothers in the conflict, but many have been led to the work only by that broader sympathy which includes all their patriotic countrymen as kinsmen in the cause of liberty.

The history and labors of each are full of interest and pathos, but we cannot give them. Of one, a woman of rare gifts, and extraordinary culture, young and gentle, and of one of the noblest and best families of Massachusetts, we may say, that from the day after the battle of Bull Run, when she pressed the hands of the wounded soldiers of that fight, in an agony of distress not less than their own, and with streaming eyes ministered to their necessities, up to the present time—in all the battles of Virginia and Maryland, and later, in the deep sands, and under the burning sun of Morris Island, amid the thunders of the bombardment of Fort Sumter, and the terrible slaughter in the assaults on Wagner—her whole thoughts, time, and energies, have been given to the care and help of the sick and wounded soldiers of our country, and nothing has been able to draw her from this blessed work.

Of another, a matron of high social

position, it may be said, that on the Peninsula and at Harrison's Landing, before Washington, at South Mountain, and Antietam, at Fredericksburg, Chancellorsville, and Gettysburg; and later still, after the battles of Chickamauga and Chattanooga, she has toiled as few women could have done, to cheer the spirits and to soothe the anguish of the soldier, to give spiritual instruction and consolation to the dying, and to lead them to the source of all comfort. She has encountered perils and dangers, from which most women would have shrunk; has become familiar with the horrors of war, whether exhibited on the field of carnage or in the crowded hospital; has more than once made her way, with garments soaked in human gore, through the long lines of wounded and dying soldiers, kneeling by the side of each, to impart some word of comfort, or to wipe the death-damps from their brows. Amid all these scenes, she retains the modesty, the retiring diffidence, and the unwillingness to speak of herself, or her labors, which characterizes the true heroine.

There are others, and many of them, as deserving, perhaps, of a record in our pages for their sacrifices and labors, but our limits do not permit us to name them here. Of all of them, it may be said as of her who anointed the Saviour's feet, "she hath done what she could."

CHAPTER VII.

CONTRIBUTIONS AND LABORS IN BEHALF OF THE FREEDMEN. —SOCIETIES ORGANIZED FOR THEIR RELIEF AND INSTRUCTION.—THE FREEDMEN'S BUREAU AT WASHINGTON.—THE PERSECUTION OF PEOPLE OF COLOR IN NEW YORK DURING THE JULY RIOTS.—PROMPT AND LIBERAL REPARATIONS MADE BY VOLUNTARY CONTRIBUTIONS OF CITIZENS.—FUNDS ALSO RAISED FOR POLICE WHO HAD AIDED IN PUTTING DOWN THE RIOT.—THE WHITE REFUGEES AND THEIR NEEDS.

THE claims of another class, reduced to destitution by the war, to be relieved, were beginning to press upon the consideration of the charitable. In those sections of the Southern States, invaded and occupied by our troops, the slaveholders, when compelled, from their active participation in the rebellion, to abandon their estates, left, for the most part, the feeble and infirm slaves upon their plantations—the old or sickly women, and the young children—and compelled the able-bodied slaves, the "prime hands," as they were called, to go with them to the interior, or sold them in the States where slavery was yet regarded as safe. Many of these afterward escaped, and came into the employ of the Union forces in various capacities. But the feeble and infirm could not be suffered to perish; and arrangements were made, under Government direction, to employ such of them as were able to work, on the plantations which had been abandoned, or in work in the vicinity of the camps, and to allow moderate rations for their sustenance. It was found, however, very soon, that they needed clothing, superintendence, schools for the children, &c., &c.; and while, so far as they were able, they were willing to pay moderate prices for these supplies, a considerable portion must be donated. Freedmen's Relief Societies were accordingly organized in Boston, New York, Philadelphia, Cincinnati, Chicago and St. Louis; and clothing, agricultural implements, books of instruction, &c., &c., forwarded to them. The

Bible and religious publication societies appropriated large numbers of simple reading books, primers, and Testaments for their use, and the Missionary Societies, as well as the Freedmen's Relief Societies, sent teachers and missionaries among them. Schools were opened for all who would attend (and this included nearly all the freedmen, from three years old to eighty), at Washington, Norfolk, Newbern, Hilton Head, Beaufort, Fernandina, New Orleans, Vicksburg, Milliken's Bend, Memphis, and elsewhere. In this work the Western Sanitary Commission has borne a noble part. Its President, Judge Yeatman has for more than six months past devoted almost his whole time to the investigation of their condition and wants and to devise means for their employment at fair wages, and with humane treatment. In January of the present year, he prepared, in connection with Mr. Mellen, agent of the Treasury Department, such regulations for leasing abandoned plantations, as will secure to the freedmen just compensation and kind care, In the autumn of 1863, special contributions of clothing, &c., were solicited for the thousands of freedmen and their families, in the Mississippi Valley, who were too old and infirm, or too young, to be able to work (the able bodied men and women having been either employed in the army or driven off by their rebel masters). The appeal was made at the instance of Gen. Grant, and met with a hearty and gratifying response. In all about $382,000 have been contributed for the relief and instruction of the freedmen.

The large numbers of emancipated slaves who have come into our lines since the promulgation of the President's proclamation, and their docility and eagerness to do all they can for their own support, and for the Government which has emancipated them, has rendered a special Department of Government necessary for the management of affairs connected with them. The Freedmen's Relief Societies have accordingly urged the erection of a Freedmen's Bureau upon Congress, and a bill for its organization is now before that body.

In July, 1863, a mob, composed principally of the most degraded portion of the population, ravaged New York for four days, committing highway robbery, arson, and murder at will. The pretext for their atrocious brutality was the attempted enforcement of the draft; the real motive which actuated their leaders was hostility to the Government. This mob were guilty of the most horrible acts of cruelty toward the people of color of the city. Peaceable, unoffending negroes were hung, drowned, beaten to death, and their houses sacked and burned by these incarnate fiends. This cruel persecution of a quiet and inoffensive people induced a decided reaction of feeling in their favor on the part of the citizens generally. The sum of $42,600, beside clothing to the value of many thousands of dollars, was promptly contributed for their relief, and $55,000 more was subscribed for the benefit of the policemen or their families who had been injured in putting down the riot. Other contributions to a considerable amount were subsequently made for the relief of the colored children and others who were sufferers by the riots.

The Unionists of the Southern States, many of whom had suffered everything but death, and thousands death itself, at the hands of the rebels, also claimed Christian charity and aid at the hands of their brethren at the North. They were deserving of it; many of them had adhered, with a love stronger than death, to the old flag, and had been loyal when all around them were drawn away by the specious pleas of the leaders of the rebellion. They had taken calmly, even joyfully, the spoiling of their goods, and had welcomed most heartily the advent of the Army of Freedom ; but intensely loyal as they were, they were naked and starving, and the relief which the army could afford them was but slight. The appeals made in their behalf were responded to with cheerfulness, and in New York, Boston, and Philadelphia nearly $150,000 in money and clothing, in large amounts, were contributed to their relief. The Government has taken measures to supply, as far as practicable, the more urgent wants of these deserving citizens, and to mitigate their sufferings.

CHAPTER VIII.

AID TO SUFFERERS IN FOREIGN COUNTRIES.—THE LANCASHIRE AND DERBYSHIRE OPERATIVES.—THE IRISH SUFFERERS.–THE FRENCH OPERATIVES.—OTHER MOVEMENTS OF PHILANTHROPY.—THE ALLOTMENT SYSTEM IN THE ARMY.—THE NATIONAL CEMETERIES AT GETTYSBURG, CHATTANOOGA, STONE RIVER, AND ANTIETAM.—THE IMPULSE GIVEN TO HOME AND FOREIGN MISSIONARY OPERATIONS AND TO OTHER BENEVOLENT ENTERPRISES.—THE CANCELING OF CHURCH DEBTS, RAISING OF CLERGYMEN'S SALARIES, ERECTION OF NEW CHURCHES, &C., &C.—CONCLUSION.

THERE was still another appeal to the sympathies of the nation, and this time from over the sea. The sudden falling off of imports from England and France, at the commencement of the war, leaving many of the manufacturers, for a time, without a market for their goods, occasioned much embarrassment and many failures among them; and before the surplus of goods had been exhausted, the rapid rise in the price of cotton, resulting from the necessary state of blockade, rendered production unprofitable, and the subsequent scarcity of that staple made it impossible to keep the mills employed. Under these circumstances, nearly four hundred thousand of the operatives in the cotton mills of Lancashire and Derbyshire, and those dependent upon them, were thrown out of employment, and soon began to suffer from starvation. They bore up bravely under their privations as long as it was possible; and fully satisfied that the war in this country to put down a rebellion caused by, and based upon slavery, was a just one, they steadily refused to throw the blame of their sufferings upon the United States Government, though often solicited to do so by English sympathizers with the South. Their condition was daily growing more desperate; and though subscriptions for their relief were made in England to the amount of $9,000,000 or $10,000,000, there was still a large amount of suffering to be relieved. The loyal American people felt that it was due to themselves that they should manifest their hearty sympathy with their brethren in distress, especially since that distress had grown, in part at least, out of the inevitable consequences of the war, and those who were the chief sufferers from it had been their firm friends under the most trying circumstances. The movement for sending aid to them was hailed with joy in al quarters; contributions poured in from all the principal cities, and from country towns as well.

An eminent shipping house offered a new and capacious vessel, to bear the gifts of the nation to England; it was soon freighted and dispatched, but could not carry all that was offered. The Corn Exchange freighted (in part) another vessel, and a considerable amount was forwarded in bills of exchange. Philadelphia also contributed a ship-load of provisions to these sufferers. The aggregate amount contributed for the relief of the Lancashire and Derbyshire operatives, was about $252,000. A few thousand dollars were also contributed for the French operatives of the Department of Seine Inferieure, Rouen, &c., who were suffering, though in a less degree.

But the charities of the nation did not stop here. No sooner were supplies forwarded to the English operatives, than it was found that extensive suffering and incipient starvation were threatening a large portion of the manufacturing districts in Ireland, and that but little aid was bestowed upon them by the English Government or people. The Irish people were bound to us by strong ties; they had offered their services freely for the war, and on every battle-field they had proved their valor and shed their blood. We could not turn a deaf ear to their appeals for help, and again, and up to the present time, contributions have flowed in liberally for their assistance, and more than $120,000 have been raised for their relief.

Our volunteer soldiers have not been unmindful of the responsibilities which the nation's trust and large-hearted liberality has imposed on them. An Act of Congress has been passed providing that the soldier may, under certain regulations which render fraud impossible, allot such portion of his pay as he desires for the benefit of his family, or those dependent upon him; and in several of the States, citizens of the highest character and standing have given their services without fee or reward as commissioners, to visit the regiments, and procure from the men allotments for their families. In the State of New York, as a result of this effort, over $8,000,000 per annum is thus forwarded to soldiers' families; in several of the other States, the amount, though smaller, is in about the same proportion to troops they have in the field. In the aggregate, more than $25,000,000 per annum is thus saved from the greed of the sutlers, or the rapacity of the gamblers, and other harpies, who always follow an army to plunder its soldiers.

The proposition to consecrate a National Cemetery for the heroes who fell at Gettysburg, was welcomed most heartily throughout the loyal States, and the Legislatures of the several States, as well as citizens in all quarters, have contributed liberally to the fund necessary for its completion and adornment; and similar measures are in progress for gathering, in appropriate graves, with the only honors a nation can bestow, the gallant dead of Antietam, Stone River, and Chattanooga. On the monuments which shall crown those heights, and stand as sentinels over the mighty and heroic dead, future ages shall read the names of those who loved their country's honor and freedom better than life.

Amid all these demands upon the liberality of a noble and generous people, it is a fact of deep interest, that no one of the charitable organizations of a peaceful time has been stinted; the orphan asylums, homes for the friendless, asylums for the aged and indigent, the dispensaries, infirmaries, and hospitals, the associations for the relief of the poor, and all those charities which have their claims upon the public, alike in times of peace and war, have been abundantly supported, and many new ones for the relief and maintenance of the children of deceased or disabled soldiers, or for giving to the crippled soldier himself a home, where he may spend the evening of life in quiet and comfort, have sprung up, and received large contributions. The great religious societies, whether national or denominational, have had a larger income than in times of peace; schools and colleges have been amply supported, and many of the latter liberally endowed;* the salaries of

* Yale College has received endowments to the amount of more than half a million of dollars since the commencement of the war, and many other colleges and universities sums varying from $50,000 to $300,000.

the clergy have been very generally increased, and in hundreds of instances debts, which had crippled the activity and impaired the usefulness of churches and congregations, have been paid off during the past year.

In this hasty sketch of the charities evoked by the war, we have necessarily omitted all mention of many of the active organizations which have devoted themselves to the welfare of the soldiers; and have, of course, been unable to give even an approximate statement of the vast amount contributed directly by individuals to the objects of their beneficence. We have, however, as we believe, demonstrated conclusively, that, neither in ancient nor modern times, has there been so vast an outpouring of a nation's wealth for the care, the comfort, and the physical and moral welfare of those who have fought the nation's battles or been the sufferers from its condition of war.

While then, in this regard, the record of the United States is one which confers the highest honor upon its humanity, its philanthropy, and its patriotism, it is yet, when viewed aright, no matter of surprise that the national heart should have been thus stirred to its innermost depths; for never, in the history of the human race, was there a rebellion so utterly unjustifiable in its character; or which, aiming at the subversion of a benign Government, only that it might rear upon its ruins a despotism, having slavery for its corner-stone, was so well calculated to call forth the scorn and abhorrence of all good and honorable men.

STATISTICAL TABLES.

NOTE.—In the following Statistical Tables it has been necessary, in some instances, to estimate the amounts contributed by small societies, individuals, &c., in the aggregate. Wherever this has been necessary, it has only been done after the most careful inquiry and investigation, and a comparison of the views of cautious and well-informed persons, and the lowest estimate has invariably been taken. It is believed, therefore, that the amounts are, in nearly every case, below the actual sums contributed.

Tabular Statement of the Contributions for various purposes, connected, directly or indirectly, with the War, to February, 1864.

I. *Amount expended by the States for the equipment and maintenance of troops not reimbursed, or guaranteed to be reimbursed, by the General Government:*		AGGREGATE.
Maine	$40,000 00	
New Hampshire (estimated)	60,000 00	
Vermont	75,000 00	
Massachusetts	1,963,311 88	
Rhode Island	605,847 74	
Connecticut	392,900 94	
New York	3,340,943 00	
New Jersey (estimated)	251,320 03	
Pennsylvania	1,448,000 00	
Ohio (estimated)	1,600,000 00	
Indiana	450,000 00	
Wisconsin	250,000 00	
Iowa	420,000 00	
Kansas	40,000 00	
Carried forward		$10,937,323 59

		AGGREGATE.
Brought forward..........	....	$10,937,323 59
II. *Bounties, Extra Pay, and Allowance to Families of Volunteers, made by States:*		
Maine.........................	$4,000,000 00	
New Hampshire (estimated).....	1,225,000 00	
Vermont.......................	2,000,000 00	
Massachusetts.................	7,625,436 00	
Rhode Island..................	2,668,350 00	
Connecticut...................	4,169,767 84	
New York......................	13,562,947 00	
New Jersey (estimated).........	1,800,000 00	
Maryland......................	100,000 00	
Ohio..........................	5,000,000 00	
Indiana.......................	3,000,000 00	
Michigan......................	1,400,000 00	
Wisconsin.....................	720,000 00	
Iowa..........................	314,000 00	
		47,585,500 84
III. *Moneys contributed by Cities, Towns, Corporations, and Individuals, for raising and recruiting regiments, aside from bounties and relief to Families:*		
In 1861.......................	7,120,000 00	
In 1862.......................	16,150,000 00	
In 1863.......................	8,360,000 00	
In January and February, 1864...	2,600,000 00	
		34,230,000 00
IV. *Bounties and Aid to Families of Volunteers, contributed by Counties, Towns, Cities, Corporations, and Individuals in each State:*		
Maine (estimated)...............	1,260,000 00	
New Hampshire..................	860,000 00	
Vermont........................	,000,000 00	
Massachusetts..................	1,815,285 30	
Rhode Island...................	943,825 06	
Connecticut....................	3,746,360 00	
Carried forward..........	$10,625,470 36	$92,752,824 43

		AGGREGATE.
Brought forward	$10,625,470 36	$92,752,824 43
New York	27,155,272 83	
New Jersey (estimated)	4,300,000 00	
Pennsylvania (of which Philadelphia contributed over five million dollars)	12,200,000 00	
Delaware	60,000 00	
Maryland	800,000 00	
Ohio (estimated)	10,750,000 00	
Indiana	3,500,000 00	
Illinois	4,720,000 00	
Michigan (estimated)	1,350,000 00	
Wisconsin	2,135,000 00	
Iowa	1,250,000 00	
Minnesota (estimated)	150,000 00	
Missouri (estimated)	500,000 00	
Kansas	100,000 00	
		79,595,743 19
V. *State Contributions for Sick and Wounded Soldiers, Governors' Contingent Fund or Special Appropriations.*		
Maine	$25,000 00	
Vermont	40,000 00	
Massachusetts	35,400 00	
Connecticut	28,641 00	
New York	250,000 00	
Maryland	10,000 00	
Indiana	100,000 00	
Illinois	69,000 00	
Michigan	48,000 00	
Wisconsin	40,000 00	
Iowa	100,000 00	
Minnesota (estimated)	20 000 00	
Missouri	50,000 00	
		816,041 00
VI. *Contributions of States to National Defense, not included under any of the foregoing heads:*		
Maine, for harbor defenses	$200,000 00	
Carried forward	$200,000 00	$173,164,608 62

		Aggregate.
Brought forward..........	$200,000 00	$173,164,608 62
Massachusetts, for harbor and coast defenses, and State war vessels	1,500,000 00	
New York, for harbor defenses, &c.	1,000,000 00	
Pennsylvania, for harbor defenses and protection from invasion..	3,500,000 00	
Ohio, for protection of river line..	1,800,000 00	
Indiana, for State Legion.........	140,000 00	
Maryland, for Home Guards, and to repel invasion..............	700,000 00	
Kentucky, for Home Guards, &c..	1,000,000 00	
Missouri, for Home Guards and State Militia..................	2,500,000 00	
Iowa, for border defense.........	200,000 00	
Minnesota, for defense against Indians........................	500,000 00	
		13,040,000 00
VII. *Contributions by Individuals or Associations, for the general purposes of National Defense, &c., not enumerated above*		
Cornelius Vanderbilt, New York. The steamship "Vanderbilt" presented to the Government—Appraised value...............	$800,000 00	
W. H. Aspinwall—Commissions presented to the Government..	25,000 00	
Other individuals—Commissions, &c., donated..................	30,000 00	
Loyal Leagues—Cash raised for organization of colored regiments, &c...	150,000 00	
		1,005,000 00
Total contributions from States, counties, towns, cities, corporations, and individuals, for aid and relief of soldiers and their families, and for purposes of national defense, not reimbursed, or to be reimbursed, by the General Government..............	....	$187,209.608 62

VIII. *Contributions for the Care and Comfort of Soldiers, whether in Camp, or Sick and Wounded, and for their Families, from Associations and Individuals:*		AGGREGATE.
United States Sanitary Commission, in money........	$1,33,628 28	
Receipts from fairs in Brooklyn, Albany, Poughkeepsie, and Yonkers, not yet paid over—about..	550,000 00	
United States Sanitary Commission—Supplies—estimated value	7,000,000 00	
Philadelphia Branch of Sanitary Commission, not included in above........................	135,000 00	
Cincinnati Branch, not included in above, about..................	300,000 00	
Northwestern Sanitary Commission (Chicago Branch).........	130,000 00	
Western Sanitary Commission—in money and supplies, estimated value by officers of Commission	1,750,000 00	
Iowa State Sanitary Commission—money and supplies...........	175,500 00	
Indiana State Sanitary Commission—money and supplies......	320,000 00	
Illinois Commissioner-General—money and supplies...........	450,000 00	
United States Christian Commission—in money............ .	400,000 00	
United States Christian Commission—supplies................	700,748 36	
New England Soldiers' Relief Association—money	28,000 00	
New England Soldiers' Relief Association—supplies............	200,000 00	
Ladies' Aid Society, Philadelphia—money	19,380 00	
Ladies' Aid Society, Philadelphia—supplies at Home Office, and sent to Secretary in the field...	210,000 00	
Soldiers' Aid Society, of Hartford, Connecticut—money and supplies	75,000 00	
Carried forward...........	$13,569,256 64	

		AGGREGATE.
Brought forward......	$13,569,256 64	
Union Relief Association, of Baltimore, and other Baltimore associations—in money............	80,000 00	
Union Relief Association, of Baltimore, &c.—supplies...........	170,000 00	
State Relief Associations at Washington—money and supplies....	1,030,000 00	
Other relief associations, East and West, not connected with the national organizations (estimated)	1,200,000 00	
Union Volunteer Refreshment Saloon, Philadelphia—money....	40,000 00	
Union Volunteer Refreshment Saloon, Philadelphia—supplies...	17,000 00	
Cooper Shop Refreshment Saloon, Philadelphia—money..........	40,232 22	
Cooper Shop Refreshment Saloon, Philadelphia—supplies.........	15,000 00	
Subsistence Committee, Pittsburgh—money and supplies....	35,000 00	
Citizens' Volunteer Hospital, Philadelphia—money, labor, and supplies........................	23,047 25	
State Soldiers' Depot, New York city—money.................	60,000 00	
State Soldiers' Depot, New York city—supplies	10,000 00	
Other Soldiers' Homes, Rests, &c., not connected with the Sanitary Commissions, in the principal cities......................	160,000 00	
American Bible Society and its auxiliaries, bibles and testaments distributed to soldiers and to rebels	300,000 00	
American Tract Society, New York, for books and tracts distributed to soldiers, and services of Missionaries and colporteurs......................	100,000 00	
American Tract Society, Boston, for books and tracts distributed to soldiers, and services of Missionaries and colporteurs......	70,229 85	
Carried forward............	$16,920,765 96	

		AGGREGATE.
Brought forward	$10,920,765 96	
Other religious societies, Missionaries and publications	125,000 00	
Supplies and money distributed to armies in Virginia and the department of the South, and to hospitals in Washington, through individuals not connected with any of the National organizations	1,350,000 00	
Money for postage, stationery, newspapers, books, and supplies, distributed to hospitals by private individuals not connected with National organizations	1,200,000 00	
Supplies and money forwarded to Western armies, camps, and hospitals, directly from towns, cities, and villages, and not passing through other organizations	4,000,000 00	
Ambulances for sick and wounded, built and maintained by Philadelphia firemen	20,000 00	
Asylums and homes for disabled soldiers and for children of deceased soldiers in New York and elsewhere	220,000 00	
Young Men's Christian Associations, aside from contributions through the Christian Commission	128,000 00	
Board of Trade, Chicago, for "Board of Trade Regiments"	65,000 00	
State Military Agents, in New York and Philadelphia	12,000 00	
Expenses in procuring the passage of the Ambulance Corps Bill	3,500 00	
Total of contributions for care and comfort of soldiers by associations and individuals	....	$24,044,865 96

		AGGREGATE.
IX. *Contributions for Sufferers abroad.*		
International Relief Fund, New York, for Lancashire sufferers..	$132,140 74	
Corn Exchange Fund, for Lancashire sufferers	60,000 00	
Philadelphia contributions for Lancashire sufferers...........	60,000 00	
Relief of French operatives	8,000 00	
Ship-load of provisions for Irish sufferers, contributed by A. T. Stewart, New York............	30,000 00	
Contributions for Irish relief, in New York....................	30,000 00	
Contributions for Irish relief, in Brooklyn....................	15,000 00	
Contributions for Irish relief, elsewhere......................	45,000 00	
		$380,140 74
X. *Contributions for Freedmen, Sufferers from the Riots, and White Refugees.*		
Freedmen's Relief Association, New York—money and supplies	$172,144 13	
Other Freedmen's Relief Associations and contributions........	150,000 00	
Aid to Freedmen by Missionary Societies, &c.................	60,000 00	
Amount contributed to Merchants' Committee, New York, for relief of colored persons injured or robbed during the New York riots.........................	42,600 00	
Amount contributed for Police injured in the riots	55,000 00	
Aid to white Union refugees from the South......	150,000 00	
		$639,644 13

Recapitulation.		Aggregate.
Total contributions from States, counties, towns, &c., for aid and relief of soldiers and their families, and for purposes of National defense....................	$187,209,608 62	
Total contributions for care and comfort of soldiers, &c., by associations and individuals.....	24,044,865 96	
Contributions for sufferers abroad.	380,140 74	
Contributions for Freedmen, sufferers from the riots, and white refugees......................	639,644 13	
Amount of Philanthropic Results of War.....................	....	$212,274,259 45

www.ingramcontent.com/pod-product-compliance
Lightning Source LLC
LaVergne TN
LVHW021404110826
845150LV00007B/1781

* 9 7 8 1 4 2 5 5 1 2 2 5 5 *